Macbeth

William Shakespeare

Guide written by Stewart Martin

A Literature Guide for GCSE

Contents

LADY MACBETH DRIVES HER HUSBAND TO MURDER.

WE'LL NOT FAIL.

IS THIS A DAGGER I SEE BEFORE ME?

KING DUNCAN IS DEAD...

OUR ROYAL MASTER IS MURDERED!

HIS SONS FLEE...

I'LL TO ENGLAND

TO IRELAND!

...AND MACBETH BECOMES KING.

MACBETH PLOTS BANQUO'S MURDER

FLY, GOOD FLEANCE

BUT IS TORMENTED BY HIS GHOST.

MACBETH TURNS TO THE WITCHES FOR GUIDANCE.

BEWARE MACDUFF!

GREAT BIRNAM WOOD..

NONE OF WOMAN BORN!

Macbeth

In Act 1, Macbeth is a <u>successful</u> general, described as <u>noble,</u> <u>valiant</u> and <u>'brave'</u>, and <u>respected</u> by his king and his fellow soldiers. He has a significant flaw in his nature, however – <u>ambition</u>. This leads him to kill the rightful King of Scotland, and the <u>evil</u> of this murder has powerful effects on him and the whole country. Macbeth knows that what he does is evil and initially is thrown into a moral quandary, but eventually the <u>temptation</u> is too strong. The witches play upon Macbeth's weakness and so does his equally ambitious wife, Lady Macbeth. Macbeth thinks that the supernatural powers of the witches will help him, but instead they lead him to ruin. Macbeth's downfall is really his own fault, because he makes a <u>deliberate</u> <u>choice</u> to take the road to evil. He is <u>responsible</u> for the murder of King Duncan, his two sleeping guards, his colleague Banquo, Lady Macduff and her children and Young Siward.

At the end of the play, Macbeth has changed from the <u>'Noble Macbeth'</u> he was at the start, to a <u>'butcher'</u> and a <u>'bloody</u> <u>tyrant'</u> hated by everyone. Macbeth is, however, a strong character and is fully aware of the good he has rejected. He is a fascinating character because he is much more than just a horrible monster. It is possible to feel repelled by the evil in Macbeth and at the same time to feel sorry for the waste of all the good things in his character.

The play has a tight, compact structure and all the action centres on Macbeth. We are granted access to his thoughts through a series of illuminating <u>soliloquies</u> in which he shares his dilemma and future plans with the audience. As a result, we feel very close to this protagonist.

You could think of Macbeth as someone who is too suspicious of those he should have trusted and too trusting of the witches, whom he should have suspected more. Or perhaps he is a terrified man trying to escape from his own conscience. Some people have interpreted Macbeth as a brave soldier who is also a moral coward. When making up your own mind, it may help to think of how Macbeth may have been seen by Banquo, Lady Macbeth or Macduff.

Lady Macbeth

Lady Macbeth is Macbeth's wife. At the start of the play she seems to have a <u>very</u> <u>strong</u> <u>character</u> – stronger even than Macbeth's, for she <u>persuades</u> him to go against his nature and better judgement. However, by the end she is <u>reduced</u> to a pitiful figure, afraid of the dark. At the beginning she is Macbeth's '<u>dearest partner</u> <u>of</u> <u>greatness</u>', but at the end she is his '<u>fiend-like</u> <u>queen</u>'.

It can be tempting to see Lady Macbeth as a traditional <u>villainess</u>, and certainly she has a lust for power. It is her goading that leads Macbeth to seize the throne of Scotland by murdering King Duncan. However, while she can talk in a brutal and aggressive way about murdering her own baby, she cannot bring herself to murder the king herself because he reminds her of her own father. This detail is <u>sentimental</u> and suggests, perhaps, that Lady Macbeth is all words. She can brag and bluster, but action defeats her. By the end of the play, Lady Macbeth is shown to be <u>unable</u> <u>to</u> <u>cope</u> with the evil she has unleashed. Macbeth begins to cut her out of his plans very quickly and, left ignorant and alone to deal with her mental anguish, she goes <u>insane</u>.

Lady Macbeth is often seen as a <u>symbol</u> <u>of</u> <u>evil</u>, like the witches, but at the end she has become its <u>victim</u>, just like her husband. It seems doubly pitiful that, even in death, her desperate attempt to find rest and eternal sleep eludes her. It is suggested that she commits suicide, and traditionally this would have meant that her soul was not saved. She would have been destined to wander forever in purgatory.

Banquo

Banquo is a loyal and honourable Scottish nobleman who is with Macbeth when he first meets the witches. Banquo senses that the witches are evil and is deeply suspicious of their powers. The witches predict that Banquo will father a line of rulers, although he will not be one himself, and that he is 'Lesser than Macbeth, and greater'.

Despite their friendship, Macbeth comes to fear Banquo's honesty and has him murdered. A question that remains unanswered about Banquo is whether this wise and moral man should – or could – have taken action when he realised that Macbeth was involved in the king's murder. His silence after Duncan's corpse is found is rather telling, and later his words are chilling: 'I fear/Thou play'dst most foully'. Banquo's ghost haunts Macbeth with the continual reminder that Banquo's children will be the rightful monarchs. Perhaps this is his way of redressing the action he should have taken earlier on in the play.

Duncan

Duncan is the rightful King of Scotland who is murdered by Macbeth for his throne. He is noble, well-respected, dignified and appreciative of loyalty in others. Duncan is generous and trusting of the people around him – perhaps too trusting – especially of the two Thanes of Cawdor, both of whom betray him. Although we only see him in Act 1, Duncan is an important <u>symbol</u> of all the things which Macbeth overthrows and destroys. He represents the <u>divine</u> <u>right</u> <u>of</u> <u>kings</u> to rule, and although in real Scottish history Duncan was a feeble and weak king, in this play he is presented as a wise and honourable ruler.

Macduff

Macduff is one of the few characters who instantly believes Macbeth to be Duncan's murderer. He certainly does not consider Macbeth fit to be a king and, dramatically, refuses to attend his coronation. Macduff is a <u>shrewd</u> man who rejects belief in the powers of witchcraft. His conversation with Malcolm shows him to be <u>honourable,</u> <u>loyal</u> and <u>patriotic</u> and his reaction to the slaughter of his family reveals his <u>tender</u> feelings as a husband and father. In many ways he is presented as the <u>dramatic</u> <u>opposite</u> to the character of Macbeth. Macduff is a 'real man', who vows revenge in the traditional fashion but is generally opposed to unnecessary bloodshed.

Interestingly, Macduff takes little part in the action until the final stages, but he is trusted by Duncan and discovers the body of the dead king. He immediately cuts himself off from any cooperation with Macbeth, avoiding the royal court. When he returns from England he helps to secure the throne for Malcolm by slaying Macbeth in hand-to-hand combat.

The witches

The witches are the physical embodiment of <u>evil</u> in the play. They are described as odd male/female creatures that look inhuman, they are insubstantial like air, and they have the power to create storms, cause wrecks at sea and disappear at will. They represent the supernatural world and dark temptation.

The world of the witches is terrifying and their language is full of spitefulness, violence and grisly references to mutilation. The witches never tell lies but, because they speak in puzzling riddles, it is possible for Macbeth to hear only what he wants to hear.

In Shakespeare's day there was widespread belief in the supernatural world and the existence of witches, but people were also starting to question many of the older ideas and beliefs about supernatural things. This uncertainty is reflected in the play; we are never quite sure whether the witches have any real power or whether they can only persuade others by suggesting things to them. The nature of the witches and their powers is ambiguous.

Donalbain and Malcolm

King Duncan has two sons, Donalbain and Malcolm. Malcolm is named by his father as the next king. Like his father, he values bravery and loyalty, but unlike him he is aware that it is possible to trust people too much. Malcolm is quick to sense the danger after Duncan's murder and so, while his brother escapes to Ireland, he flees to England. He has become shrewd and self-possessed by the time we meet him again, in England, where he tests Macduff's loyalty. He leads an army back to Scotland where, together with Macduff and other nobles, they defeat Macbeth. At the end of the play, Malcolm makes a noble speech which seems designed to convince the audience that Scotland once again has its rightful king.

Kingship and honour

Written for King James I, the play's primary focus is on kingship. The opening scenes show brave warriors fighting to stop traitors and foreign enemies seizing Scotland's throne. The main purpose of the play is to illustrate vividly what happens when men like Macbeth do not behave honourably. These men make bad kings. It is crucial to understand the significance of Duncan's murder. The implication is that the rightful king maintains the balance of order, not only in the state but in the natural world (see section on Order and Chaos). Throughout the play there are many references to the crown, which is the symbol of kingship: 'golden round', 'fruitless crown', 'murders on their crowns', 'the round and top of sovereignty' and 'gold-bound brow'.

At the end of the play, Macbeth refuses to take the honourable, 'Roman' way of dying (falling on his sword) and challenges Macduff to a duel. The fact that Macduff is the honourable man, and is fighting for the good of the rightful heir to the throne, means that he is ultimately victorious. The play ends with the line 'see us crowned at Scone'.

Evil and the supernatural

The nature and effects of evil dominate the action of the play from the mystical, eerie opening scene. Shakespeare presents the view that the potential for evil is present in nature, in man and in animals, and the play's imagery evokes this. Evil is a force, manifested literally in the supernatural shape of the three witches, but it is also present in bad omens and signs. The 'rooky wood', 'crows' and 'black bat' are all symbols of witchcraft. There are other supernatural elements: Banquo's ghost appearing to taunt Macbeth, the dagger hallucination, the apparitions conjured by the weird sisters and the unnatural events occurring in nature. Audiences would have also understood the significance of other signs of demonic possession – Macbeth cannot say 'Amen', and by the end of the play he loses his sense of fear. Aside from the terrific dramatic potential these events create, they would also have served as a moralistic warning. Meddle with the forces of right and good by embracing evil and these are the consequences.

Blood

Macbeth is a play drenched in blood. The opening scenes feature reports of Macbeth slashing his enemies in two, while the Thane of Cawdor is beheaded as punishment for his treason. After the murder of Duncan there seems to be blood everywhere: on the two daggers, smeared over the faces of the sleeping grooms, on Macbeth's hands, and Lady Macbeth wonders how the 'old man had so much blood in him'. (It is referred to both overtly and in euphemism as 'colour', 'incarnadine', 'gild' and 'red'.) After Banquo's murder, one of the hired killers appears at the banquet with blood on his face, and Banquo's ghost shakes his 'gory locks' at Macbeth. Lady Macbeth goes mad, desperately trying to wash imaginary blood from her hands. Macduff is symbolised by a 'bloody child' and, at the end of the play, calls for Macbeth's blood: 'clamorous harbingers of blood and death'. The play ends with Malcolm, of true royal blood, being rightfully crowned.

Darkness and light

Images of light are linked to innocence and purity. King Duncan says that the signs of nobility are 'like stars'. Light is a symbol of truth, openness and goodness. Macbeth and Lady Macbeth are creatures of the dark because darkness symbolises treachery, cruelty and evil. Macbeth tells the stars to hide their fires and Lady Macbeth calls up the blackest smoke of Hell to hide her actions. After Duncan has been murdered, Ross comments that 'dark night strangles the travelling lamp', and when Banquo is killed one of the murderers asks, 'Who did strike out the light?' Towards the end of the play, when Lady Macbeth is overcome by guilt, she fears the dark and needs to have a candle next to her all night. Interestingly, when Macbeth hears of her death he murmurs 'Out, out, brief candle'. Perhaps he believes that the only peace available to her is in death.

Nature

This is a strong motif in the play. Natural growth is seen as a symbol of order: there are references to the 'planting' of seeds and of people, to seeds germinating and to the goodness of things growing naturally, especially children. Under Macbeth, Scotland becomes 'drowned with weeds'. Using pathetic fallacy, elements from the natural world reveal the atmosphere at certain times in the play. Birds of prey, toads and snakes suggest a threatening atmosphere, the witches are accompanied by storms, and as soon as Macbeth seizes the throne, nature is shown to be thrown into disarray, with unnatural events occurring and the natural food chain broken. The fact that trees are mentioned so often in the play, might be a sly reference to the royal family tree. The nature motif reaches its visual and dramatic climax when Macbeth sees Birnam Wood literally uproot itself and march towards the castle. When Malcolm finally appears he is surrounded by soldiers, all carrying leafy branches. Shakespeare's point is clear – Macbeth's actions go against nature itself, and because of this, even the natural world will play its part in his final uprooting.

Appearance and reality

One of the key themes in the play is that evil lurks behind the most innocent and pleasant façade. Just because a person or a place looks attractive, does not mean it can be trusted. Lady Macbeth urges Macbeth to look like 'the innocent flower, but be the serpent under't'. She wants him to present a picture of beauty and frailty, while being ready to strike and kill. Before fleeing to Ireland, Donalbain shows great perception when he notes 'there's daggers in men's smiles'. He realises that just because things seem right on the surface, he cannot ignore the fact that someone has brutally murdered his father, and probably intends to kill him too. Significantly, Banquo comments on how pleasant Macbeth's castle is, with its perfumed air and flock of house martins. Of course this could not be further from the truth, for it becomes the gateway to Hell after Duncan's murder.

Additionally, the weird sisters are mistresses of deception and their own appearance means that Macbeth cannot initially tell whether they are humans or not. The fact that they have beards blurs their gender, and their riddles are deliberately designed to make Macbeth believe one thing when they mean something entirely different.

Order and chaos

The duality of order versus chaos runs through the play. The first scene opens against a chaotic backdrop of heavenly disorder, with thunder, lightning and a terrible storm. The witches chant that 'Fair is foul, and foul is fair' and this paradox sets the tone. Macbeth cannot tell whether the witches are on his side or not and his murder of the king plunges the country into turmoil. It is significant, too, that the witches appear after a dreadful, bloody battle, where foreign invaders were threatening the established status quo. Chaos and disorder are suggested in many ways. Nature is turned upside down after King Duncan's murder, when a falcon is killed by an owl and Duncan's horses eat each other.

People in Shakespeare's time thought that every person and thing had a natural place, decided by God. They also believed in the divine right of kings to rule. This means that Macbeth's main crime is in upsetting this natural order. He murders people so that they die before their time. He throws the political stability of Scotland into chaos and destroys his marriage and his own mental 'order'. His wife goes mad, breaking natural order again by taking her own life. In the play, loyalty to the true king and the state is shown as good, rebellion against it as bad. This is why traitors are punished with death and why it is important for the audience to witness the final single-handed combat between Macduff, representing proper order, and Macbeth who stands for evil and disorder.

Children and babies

This is an important theme because children and babies represent innocence and vulnerability. Macbeth is terrified that Banquo's children will be heirs to the throne. Ironically, Macbeth and Lady Macbeth have no children of their own, although Lady Macbeth hints that she knows how it feels to suckle a child and talks about 'dashing' out the brains of a newborn baby – words which reveal her ruthless ambition. Macbeth later has Macduff's children brutally slain, an action reinforced to the audience with many references to their youth (they are called 'fry', meaning baby fish, and 'egg'). Shakespeare also features a bloody child as one of the witches' apparitions, representing Macduff's birth by caesarian section. So children, in a way, are the cause of Macbeth's final defeat.

About the author

William Shakespeare

Although Shakespeare is probably recognised as the greatest playwright in the world, very little detail is actually known about his life. Information about him has come to us from registrar records, marriage certificates and snippets of information detailed by his rivals and fellow actors. One critic called him 'an upstart crow beautified with our feathers' and 'the only Shakes-scene in a country'.

He was born in 1564, and although we cannot be certain of his actual birthday, it is likely, and somehow fitting, that he was born on St George's Day (April 23rd) because there is evidence that he was christened three days later.

He was born in Stratford-Upon-Avon, the eldest son of John and Mary Shakespeare. We know that William's father was a town official of Stratford and a local businessman, whose trade has been described as a 'glover', because he worked with leather and produced items like purses and gloves. Shakespeare himself is often described as a keen businessman.

Despite the fact that his works are studied in virtually every school, very little is known about Shakespeare's own schooling. It is assumed that he attended the King's New Grammar School in Stratford, although there is no concrete proof of this. He would have been taught basic reading and writing, Latin and Greek history, as well as advanced rhetoric, or the art of speech-making. Certainly, there is much evidence in his plays of great skill in this latter subject. A lack of proof suggests that he almost certainly never went to university.

In 1582, when he was only 18 years old, he married the much older (and pregnant) Anne Hathaway, and by 1585 was the father of three children: a daughter and a pair of twins. Never really a family man, it is thought that around 1589 Shakespeare left his home in Stratford to pursue his writing craft in London. For seven years he virtually disappeared without trace – a time often referred to as the 'Lost Years'. It is conjectured that he may have had to flee Stratford after dicing with the law following a spot of poaching, but nothing is known for sure.

His first poem, *Venus and Adonis* was entered in the Stationers' Registrar in 1593, and two years later, pursuing his interest in the theatre, he became a shareholder in 'The Lord Chamberlain's Men', an acting company that eventually became extremely popular.

By the end of the century, 'The Globe', the company's most well-known theatre (and recently rebuilt) opened on Bankside in London. It was here that most of his plays were performed in the open air. His success meant that he was awarded an accolade by King James I in 1603, when his company was granted a royal patent. The acting troop was renamed 'The King's Men' and they played about 12 performances each year at court.

In approximately 1609, Shakespeare is believed to have returned to his family home and wife in Stratford, having been living virtually permanently in London for 20 years (despite it being only four-days' ride away and the fact that his only son was taken ill and later died in 1596).

Shakespeare himself died in 1616, probably on his birthday, and was later buried in Trinity Church in Stratford-Upon-Avon. In his will he memorably left his daughter Susannah £300 and his wife, Anne, his 'second-best bed'!

In his lifetime he wrote 37 plays and scores of sonnets and poems, and his works were performed in front of both peasants and royalty. He is credited with expanding the English language by some 3,000 words (although not all are still in use today) and his legacy is a collection of work that has never been rivalled.

Shakespeare was a fine dramatist and storyteller, but he was not a historian. He realised, however, that historical events could provide him with superb material to be transformed into plays. For *Macbeth* he looked to the historian Holinshed, who wrote *The Chronicles of England, Scotland and Ireland* in 1587.

The Scotland that Holinshed documented was a country in the eleventh century, troubled by weak leaders and violent wars and invasions. Murder and rebellion were commonplace and loyalty was easily transferred between warring lords and landowners. Macbeth was a real Scottish aristocrat, born in 1005. He was the son of a wealthy family who ruled large portions of Scotland. His own father was murdered and he eventually married Gruach, the granddaughter of the High King. As in Shakespeare's play, the Macbeths did not have any children of their own.

The real King Duncan, unlike the one presented in the play, was a weak and ineffectual ruler and many people were pleased when he was killed. Macbeth was elected to replace him in 1040 and he ruled for 17 years, 10 of which were successful.

However, because Shakespeare wrote to please his own audience, he always made changes to the sources he used. In the case of Macbeth, it suited his story to have an ambitious warrior who wrongfully displaced a good and honourable king. In Holinshed's history, there is also a suggestion that the king's murder was performed by Macbeth and Banquo together. As James I, the king on the throne during Shakespeare's life, was allegedly descended from Banquo's line, Shakespeare made very sure that his own Banquo was an innocent party. He certainly did not want to upset his king and be accused of treason – an offence punishable by death.

The witches were also added to excite and thrill a Stuart audience fascinated by the supernatural. King James, in particular, was very interested in witchcraft and in 1597 he published *Daemonologie*, a book on the subject, which he made sure was printed in London in 1603. In addition, in 1590 it had been alleged that witches had plotted to kill the king, but they were discovered and brought to trial. King James personally interrogated one of the suspects, who was subsequently horribly tortured.

In order to add contextual interest, Shakespeare also made sure that he added plenty of modern gossip and sly references to popular news stories and events in all his plays. *Macbeth* is no different, and there are many such hints and references – some from the drunken porter, but others subtly inserted elsewhere in the play. For example, in Act 1 Scene 5 Shakespeare cleverly alludes to the Gunpowder Plot of 1605. The medal minted to celebrate the defeat of the plotters showed a snake concealed by flowers: 'Look like the innocent flower, / But be the serpent under't.'

Rufus Sewell as Macbeth in the 1999, Queen's Theatre production.

Text commentary

Act I

Scene 1

> **❝** *When shall we three meet again?*
> *In thunder, lightning, or in rain?* **❞**

The play starts dramatically with thunder, lightning and the three witches. By starting the play in this way, Shakespeare leaves you in no doubt about what it is going to be about. The focus is on the **struggle between the forces of good and evil**; a struggle between light and darkness. The **violent weather** signifies from the very start that this is a time of **disorder and chaos**. It is also clear who is to be the target for the forces of evil: the witches make an appointment to meet again to lure Macbeth to destruction.

Explore

An 'oxymoron' is when two opposite ideas are placed together. The play is full of these contradictions. Can you find others as you read on?

When the witches chant '**Fair is foul, and foul is fair**' you can guess that it is going to be hard in the play to tell the difference between good and evil. The way things appear may not be the way they really are. Things that look good may turn out to be evil, evil things may seem to be good; just like some characters in the play. The notion of **appearance and reality** and the ease with which some characters are deceived is a key theme running through *Macbeth*.

Greymalkin and Paddock are the witches' familiars, demon-companions in animal form, usually cats or toads. The fact that Macbeth is the only other name mentioned might indicate that he, too, will become a kind of **pet** for the witches.

Scene 2

The Captain tells Duncan about the **bravery** of Macbeth and Banquo. They are in **command** of the army that is fighting off an invasion. King Duncan is grateful and makes Macbeth Thane (Lord) of Cawdor.

❝ *The victory fell on us* ❞

King Duncan's first words in the play are: '**What bloody man is that?**' Duncan is referring to the Captain, who is bleeding because he has come straight from battle. The recurring image of **spilled blood** appears a lot in the play. It is ironic that Duncan should mention it first. Macbeth is ambitious to become king and will soon make a 'bloody man' out of Duncan.

Explore

Macbeth is referred to as 'Bellona's bridegroom'. Bellona was the Roman goddess of war. What does this say about Macbeth and why might this be even more significant when we see his relationship with his wife?

The loyalty and bravery of Macbeth and Banquo are contrasted with the **treason** and cowardice of the Thane of Cawdor, who betrayed the king and joined the enemy.

The Captain says that Macbeth and Banquo were **savage** in battle. Macbeth's savagery is praised here because it has preserved the rightful king. Nevertheless, he is described using **violent and blood-thirsty** imagery; he delivers '**bloody execution**' and splits a man in two, using his sword to 'carve' out a victory. Later on, Macbeth's savage character is condemned as evil and his viciousness overthrows the king and creates chaos in the land.

Images of blood are often connected with images of water in the play. Here, Macbeth and Banquo are said to '**bathe in reeking wounds**'. Later, Banquo will 'bathe in blood' and Macbeth will describe the blood he has shed as a river. The Captain says it was

Text commentary

as if they were trying to '**memorise** **another** **Golgotha**'. Golgotha ('the place of the skull') was where Christ was crucified. This is an interesting allusion as it links Macbeth with perhaps the most famous historical incident where goodness and holiness were destroyed, and serves to foreshadow his later ruthless actions. This scene gives a glowing picture of Macbeth and Banquo as loyal and brave.

> **❝***What he hath lost, noble Macbeth hath won***❞**

When the treacherous Thane of Cawdor is captured, the king says he must be executed, and his title is given to Macbeth. The irony is that the new Thane of Cawdor will be even more treacherous.

Explore

Make a list of words, images and comparisons used to describe and glorify Macbeth. What impression are we given of him, so far?

According to the Captain, Macbeth and Banquo have triumphed over two armies: that of the rebel Macdonwald and that of the Norwegian king, Sweno, assisted by the traitor Cawdor. This is the first mention of the idea of **dishonour**. As in Act 5 (when Macbeth is the king under attack), there is a union of discontented Scots and a foreign army.

Note that the scene is structured around two messenger speeches, both full of ornate vocabulary and images praising Macbeth's valour: the first by the Captain, the second by Ross.

Scene 3

> **❝***That look not like inhabitants of the earth***❞**

Macbeth and Banquo are returning from the battle when they meet the three witches who predict that Macbeth will be king and that Banquo will be the father of many kings.

One of the witches describes how she will **punish** a sailor (the Pilot) because his wife would not give her some of the chestnuts she was eating. This shows how **spiteful** the witches are and how they can do a lot of harm. The witch is not powerful enough to sink the ship, but she can make sure it is tossed about in stormy seas, and will torment the Pilot so that he cannot sleep. The ship is a **metaphor** (a figure of speech) for the ship of state and represents Scotland, which is going to suffer a 'storm' when Macbeth is its Pilot. This scene further develops the idea of tempestuous weather. The witches can only create the **climate for evil**: man alone causes chaos in the world by destroying order.

Explore

The witches' scenes have a strong and distinctive rhythm and rhyme scheme. What is the effect of this do you think?

> **❝A drum, a drum, Macbeth doth come❞**

As is the case with King Duncan, the first words spoken by Macbeth are very significant. He enters to the sound of a **beating drum**, a sound effect which indicates to the audience his **growing status and importance**. He says that he has never seen '**so foul and fair a day**', meaning that the battle has been foul but their victory has been splendid. Notice how his words are **paradoxical** and **echo** those spoken earlier by the witches.

Explore

What reasons can Shakespeare have had for giving Macbeth an almost identical line to the witches?

> **❝ If you can look into the seeds of time
> And say which grain will grow and
> which will not❞**

The witches' words have a powerful effect on Macbeth. Banquo notices this and asks him if he fears their words. Banquo cannot see why this great warrior should be afraid when he is promised only good things. What the witches say seems to strike a chord in Macbeth's mind, especially the prediction that he will be king.

Banquo introduces **clothing** as one of the major images in the play. He makes a pun on 'rapt', meaning 'totally involved in', and 'wrapped', meaning 'covered' or 'enveloped in'. Banquo also calls on the witches to tell him his future and they say he will be the father of kings.

The witches vanish and Macbeth wonders if they have **disappeared into the air**: what he thought was solid has melted away. Other things around Macbeth that he thinks are solid, like his friends, loyalty, a good king on the throne and law and order in the state, will also melt away under the evil influence of the witches.

Banquo seems **suspicious** of the witches. Unlike Macbeth, he has **no hidden ambitions**. Macbeth seems **worried** about the prediction that Banquo's children will be kings, as though this is some kind of **threat** to his future. If Banquo's children will be kings, Macbeth's rise to power will be pointless if his line stops when he dies.

❝The instruments of darkness tell us truths❞

Soon after the witches vanish, Ross and Angus arrive with the news that Macbeth has been given the title **Thane of Cawdor**. Macbeth is amazed and, developing Banquo's earlier metaphor, asks them why they 'dress him in borrowed robes'. Soon he will also be wearing the stolen clothes of the king and, more literally, the crown of Scotland.

Macbeth says that 'the greatest is behind', meaning that all he has to achieve now is to become king. The word 'behind' is significant because it seems to suggest the sneaky and underhand way in which Macbeth eventually seizes the crown. He betrays Duncan's trust and metaphorically 'stabs him in the back'. He makes another mention of Banquo's children being kings and the idea seems to affect him.

Banquo advises **caution**, pointing out that the forces of evil sometimes tell people small things that will come true so that they can be deceived into believing greater things which are false. He is **less impressed** with the truth of the witches' predictions and can **see through their trickery**. Unlike Macbeth, he realises that minds can be easily deceived by clever words. Banquo recognises the witches for what they are and for the moment puts them out of his mind.

> *If chance will have me king,*
> *Why chance may crown me*

Macbeth speaks his first major soliloquy and asks himself two questions. If what the witches said was evil, why have two good things they said turned out to be true? If what the witches said was good, why does his body react so violently to their predictions? He says they '**make my seated heart knock at my ribs / Against the use of nature**'. This suggests that he understands how even having these thoughts is **upsetting the natural balance and divine order of the world**.

Notice that it is Macbeth who mentions '**murder**', whereas the witches said nothing about murdering anyone. It is Macbeth who connects the ideas of kingship and murder. At the moment, though, Macbeth thinks the idea of murder is 'fantastical', meaning that it exists only in his imagination. Macbeth decides to leave it to **chance** to decide whether he will become king or not. He uses vocabulary linked to **the mind**, with abstract nouns such as 'thought' and 'imaginings', but it is ominous and significant that his words are almost exactly the same as his description of the witches: 'Are ye fantastical?'

Banquo again talks about Macbeth being '**rapt**', this time in thought. He wonders if perhaps Macbeth's new title – Thane of Cawdor – feels strange at the moment. Banquo supposes that

Text commentary

Explore

Look at Macbeth's speeches after receiving news from Ross and Angus. What do these words reveal about his thoughts?

Macbeth will get used to his new honours and will feel more comfortable wearing them.

Throughout this scene it is fascinating to note when Macbeth speaks, when he is silent and how he speaks to different people. With the witches he is firstly struck dumb and then becomes urgent in calling after them.

Scene 4

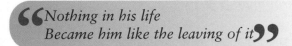

*"Nothing in his life
Became him like the leaving of it"*

Macbeth and Banquo arrive at King Duncan's court to hear of the **execution** of the treacherous Cawdor. Malcolm explains that he died in a **noble** and **honourable** fashion, confessing his crime and begging forgiveness. This detail gives an ominous foreshadowing of events and reminds the audience what end befalls traitors.

Explore

Can you find any other examples of this theme of fertility? Why do you think it is important in the play?

King Duncan says to Macbeth that he has started to '**plant**' him, meaning that he will make sure that Macbeth grows greater and stronger as a reward for his service. This is ironic because what is growing in Macbeth is the **seed** of **his** **ambition** to be king himself. When this seed grows it will lead to Duncan's death. Fertility is an important image in the play and links all the characters together. It begins with the witches looking into 'the seeds of time' and reaches a visual climax with the uprooting of Birnam Wood.

Duncan says that his eldest son, Malcolm, is to succeed him as king. It was the custom in Scotland for each king to be **elected** by the Thanes. Duncan's action is therefore unusual and this announcement comes as a shock to Macbeth, who has only recently decided to leave to chance whether or not he becomes king himself.

> **❝***That is a step / On which I must fall down,
> or else o'erleap, / For in my way it lies***❞**

Macbeth changes his mind and decides to **make his own fortune** because he now sees Duncan's son as an obstacle between himself and the throne. Macbeth makes a short speech as an aside, telling the audience his thoughts.

He admits that he has '**black and deep desires**' and calls upon the stars not to shine their light on his thoughts. This is a brief but powerful speech that gives the audience a real indication of Macbeth's evil intentions. The colour imagery is significant and carries connotations of **darkness** and the witches. It seems that Macbeth is already more than prepared to **shun the light of the pure of heart**, and open his mind to black thoughts.

To show his gratitude to Macbeth, the king says he will visit him at his castle. This is a great honour for Macbeth. It is ironic that fate seems to have given Macbeth the perfect opportunity to fulfill his ambition. He rushes to his castle to prepare for his honoured guest.

Scene 5

> **❝***My dearest partner in greatness***❞**

Lady Macbeth reads a letter from Macbeth, telling her about the meeting with the witches and Duncan's forthcoming visit. She vows to kill the king and to persuade Macbeth to join her.

Macbeth's letter is highly revealing. His version of events is accurate, but the events which he chooses to report to her all point towards the possible seizure of the throne. 'I have learnt by the perfectest report they have in them more than mortal knowledge' suggests that he is now certain the witches are right. His wife is 'his dearest partner of greatness', which indicates an equality between them. 'Greatness is promised' her. Macbeth may have pangs of conscience, Lady Macbeth may drive him on, but you should have no doubt who first has the idea of seizing power.

66 *too full o' th' milk of human kindness* 99

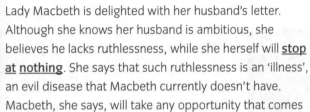

Lady Macbeth is delighted with her husband's letter. Although she knows her husband is ambitious, she believes he lacks ruthlessness, while she herself will **stop at nothing**. She says that such ruthlessness is an 'illness', an evil disease that Macbeth currently doesn't have. Macbeth, she says, will take any opportunity that comes his way, but only wants to win his honours honestly. He wants to be king even though the throne is not his by right, but he will not play falsely.

Explore

What elements of Macbeth's personality does Lady Macbeth list? How do these add to what we already know of him?

Lady Macbeth decides that she will have to help him to find the necessary determination. She reveals her intention to pour '**spirits**' in Macbeth's ear. She means she will talk to him and fill him with her own strength. The fact that she chooses this image, however, hints at a link with the supernatural and the witches. Later on she also summons 'spirits' of her own.

66 *unsex me here / And fill me from the crown to the toe topfull / Of direst cruelty* 99

A messenger comes to tell Lady Macbeth that King Duncan will arrive that night. Lady Macbeth is excited, seeing this as the perfect opportunity to make Macbeth king. In a **spell-like** soliloquy she calls up the spirits of darkness to take away her natural womanliness and to fill her instead with bitterness, poison, wickedness and cruelty. She does not want any natural

feelings of regret or conscience to get in the way of what she intends. There is a recurring image of venom and poison running through the play, as well as references to dangerous creatures such as snakes and scorpions. What does this indicate about the state of Scotland?

Like Macbeth, she asks the powers of darkness to hide her thoughts so that not even the forces of heaven can see through the 'blanket of the dark'. This is another example of the clothing image, this time meaning cloaking or hiding something so that its true nature is concealed. It is interesting that she wants to be **unsexed**. She means that she wishes to lose the gentle sensibilities associated with being feminine, but in fact this might remind us of the witches and their uncertain gender.

When Macbeth arrives to tell her that Duncan is coming to stay for one night, Lady Macbeth predicts that Duncan will never see another day's sunrise. Her plans are already made. Continuing the theme of **appearance and reality**, she tells Macbeth to deceive their guest and to hide his real thoughts. She says that people can read Macbeth's thoughts in his face. She tells him to be more like the **poisonous serpent** that lies hidden beneath the **innocent flower**. She says that Macbeth must become better at deceiving people and at being evil if he wants to achieve his ambitions.

Lady Macbeth's power at **masking** her true thoughts is clear even when talking to her husband. She uses phrases with **more than one meaning**, for example when she refers to Duncan's visit and says '**he…must be provided for**'. On one hand this could suggest that she is preparing to be a good hostess, but considering her previous soliloquy we cannot help but feel she is implying something far more sinister. There are many similar occasions in the play when words can be interpreted in several ways.

Text commentary

31

Scene 6

> **This castle hath a pleasant seat**

King Duncan arrives at Macbeth's castle with his followers, including Banquo. Duncan and Banquo talk about how pleasant a place it is to visit. They say the air '**recommends** **itself**' and '**is** **delicate**'. This is ironic in view of Lady Macbeth's words in the previous scene, and even more so when compared with what the witches said about the '**fog** **and** **filthy** **air**' surrounding their evil deeds. Banquo also refers to **summer** **birds**, such as house martins, in contrast to the death-bird **ravens** referred to by Lady Macbeth in the previous scene.

Explore

'Pathetic fallacy' is a term used when a description of nature reflects emotions. Are there any other examples in the play?

Lady Macbeth welcomes Duncan. Her words are false, but she has no difficulty in hiding her real thoughts. Her **concealment** of her motives and feelings is all part of a very formal scene: everybody is polite and complimentary. Lady Macbeth is the great **deceiver**, of course, but Banquo also seems to be happy to be there. Macbeth is already in the castle, as we know, but it is interesting to note that he is not there to welcome Duncan himself. Why do you think this is? Would Banquo have been suspicious of this?

Scene 7

> **I have no spur
> To prick the sides of my intent, but only
> Vaulting ambition which o'erleaps itself**

Macbeth cannot make up his mind whether or not to kill Duncan. He **wrestles** **with** **his** **conscience**. He says that if the murder could be done quickly, without the inevitable consequences, then he would do it. He also knows that the murder would be wrong and that he would end up

List all the reasons why Macbeth believes he should not kill the king. (Hint: There are at least seven.)

paying the price for his crime. Up till now Macbeth has been portrayed as a decisive man of action, but this is a **moral** **problem** and it makes him hesitate. Macbeth lists reasons why he should not kill the king. He is Duncan's kinsman, his host and his subject: Macbeth should therefore be the one to protect him.

Macbeth's conscience is very persuasive. He tells himself that Duncan's **goodness** and **kindness** are such that his murder would provoke a tremendous outcry. Duncan's goodness will be '**like angels, trumpet-tongued**' if he is murdered, and Macbeth will be condemned to 'deep damnation'. Shakespeare includes many images of heaven and hell – because Duncan is the **rightful king**, heaven would be outraged at his murder.

However, heaven and hell are not Macbeth's only (or even main) concern. His conscience may plague him, but his main worry is with 'this bank and shoal of time': the here and now. Duncan may be saintly, Macbeth may risk damnation, but he is prepared to 'jump' (risk) the life to come if he can get away with it in this life. The problem is that the murder of a king creates a precedent and risks the same thing happening to him – as indeed it does at the end of the play.

Macbeth admits that the only thing driving him on is his selfish ambition. Rather as Lady Macbeth did, he worries that his ambition may be greater than his ability to achieve it. He may be like a horseman who tries to vault too hastily onto his horse's back and finishes up falling off on the other side.

We will proceed no further in this business

When Lady Macbeth comes in he tells her he will not murder Duncan. He says that Duncan has given him 'new honours' which he wants to 'wear' while they are new. He sees himself 'dressed' in the good opinions of other people. This is the only reason

Macbeth gives his wife. He does not mention the many others he has just been wrestling with himself. Perhaps he does not want to admit that he has a conscience and is unhappy about doing evil. Perhaps he does not want to seem weak.

> 66 *Was the hope drunk*
> *Wherein you dressed yourself?* 99

Lady Macbeth continues the use of clothing imagery, but turns it against Macbeth. She says that he is acting as if he were drunk when he clothed himself in his hopes to be king. This suggests that he was foolish and not fully aware of his intentions. There is a suggestion that he made the decision when under the influence of a powerful drink. Of course he was intoxicated, not by alcohol, but by the witches' prophecies.

Explore

Some critics believe that this speech suggests Lady Macbeth has already had at least one child. What do you think? How might this affect her words?

Lady Macbeth accuses him of being a coward. In a **powerful** and **violent speech** she explains how far she would be prepared to go to get what she wanted. She tells him that if, like him, she had sworn to do something then, before she would go back on her word, she would tear her own baby from suckling milk at her nipple and dash its brains out. To reiterate the strength of her resolve she juxtaposes references to tenderness – 'suck', 'babe', 'milk', 'love', 'smiling' – with those of violent action – 'pluck', 'dashed'. This is another example of Lady Macbeth shunning the finer sensitivities of femininity, and the aggressive imagery suggests an almost **inhuman**, brutally masculine strength.

At this point Lady Macbeth seems to have joined the forces of evil. She has seen a chance to make her husband king and is determined not to let it slip away. She is very forceful in her language and conjures up images of brutality and horror. She seems to have been granted her earlier wish to the evil spirits to 'fill [her] from the crown to the toe top-full / Of direst cruelty'. The **horror** contained within her speech, with its reference to gruesome body parts – 'gums', 'bone', 'nipple', 'brains' – makes her seem even more **witch-like** and is echoed by the witches themselves in their deadly brew in Act 4.

> **❝Screw your courage to the sticking place❞**

Macbeth's earlier decision not to kill Duncan crumbles under the scornful attack of his wife, especially when his bravery is questioned. However, he is still worried about what will happen to them if they fail. Lady Macbeth tells him that they will not fail if he keeps his nerve. She tells Macbeth the details of her plan and he admires her determination. Developing the theme of children, he says that she should have only male children so that they would have all her courage and strength of character. This also reiterates her own masculine power and resolve.

Explore

There are many references to male and female qualities in the play. What characteristics do you associate with each gender? How are these stereotypes deliberately muddled by Shakespeare?

Manhood is a frequent theme in this scene. Lady Macbeth sees it simply: a man has courage to act and to face danger. Macbeth (lines 47–48) says that he dares to do anything that is suitable to a man; to do more would be unmanly, and possibly inhuman.

The Act ends with Macbeth finally resolved.

> **❝Away, and mock the time with fairest show; False face must hide what the false heart doth know❞**

Text commentary

Who? What? Where? When? Why? How?

1   Who is named as Duncan's successor and what title is he given?

2   Who are 'the instruments of darkness'?

3   What titles does Macbeth hold by the end of Act 1? What titles has he been promised?

4   What is unnatural about the witches' appearance?

5   Where do the witches first meet Macbeth and Banquo?

6   Why does Lady Macbeth say: 'Yet I do fear thy nature'?

7   Why is Macbeth reluctant to kill Duncan (according to his words to himself and to Lady Macbeth)?

8   How does Lady Macbeth propose to deal with Duncan's guards?

Open quotes

Find the line and complete the phrase or sentence.

1   'Stars, hide your fires...'

2   'Thou wouldst be great...'

3   'That but this blow / Might be the be-all...'

4   'I have no spur...'

5   'We fail!...'

Imperfect speakers?

The witches are called 'imperfect speakers' because their meaning seems ambiguous. Here are some early signs that ambiguity and lack of trust are major themes in the play.

1   What three apparently contradictory promises do the witches make to Banquo?

2   Why might the audience already be uneasy when the witches hail Macbeth by three titles?

3   What does Banquo suspect when the first prophecy proves true?

4   Why does Macbeth think 'This supernatural soliciting / Cannot be ill; cannot be good'?

Text commentary

Act 2

Scene 1

Briefly alone on the battlements with his son Fleance, Banquo's **concerns** and **suspicions** are evident. There is an **edginess** about his words. His sword is out in readiness and he talks of his 'cursed thoughts' that will not let him sleep.

Shakespeare often made use of scenes set on balconies or battlements because the design of the theatre meant that actors could use a real balcony. This added a sense of realism, and separated some of the action helping the audience to focus on the atmosphere.

Explore

Why can't Banquo sleep? Is he worried about the witches or does he have suspicions of how Macbeth is reacting to the prophecies?

Macbeth arrives and he and Banquo talk about the predictions of the witches. Banquo reminds Macbeth that the witches showed some of the truth to him. Macbeth now puts on the 'false face' his wife talked about and lies when he says that he has not thought about the witches' predictions at all.

> **❝Is this a dagger I see before me❞**

After Banquo and Fleance leave him, Macbeth sees a vision of a **dagger** covered in blood, with the handle pointing towards him. Macbeth speaks another **important soliloquy**. He wonders whether the dagger is inviting him to execute the murder. His mind is full of dark thoughts and this fearless soldier is now tormented by images of blood and fear of the unknown.

His words are filled with references to evil and witchcraft – 'wicked dreams', 'Hecate', 'howl', 'ghost', 'horror' – which show how much his mind has been tainted by the weird sisters. This kind of killing goes against Macbeth's nature and <u>against natural law</u>. Macbeth says that across half the world (the half in the darkness of night) nature 'seems dead'. The <u>darkness</u> is a symbol of the way evil powers are rising up to strike at the powers of goodness and light. Macbeth wonders whether he is going insane.

Explore

How would you stage this difficult scene if you were the director? Would you have the dagger as a visible object or would you use other techniques to suggest Macbeth's hallucination?

The dagger is the first of several visions shown to Macbeth. He cannot tell whether they are real or imaginary. They are symbols of the power of evil spirits in the world and of the evil that is growing in his own heart. As a bell rings (in funeral tones) he goes to carry out the murder.

Macbeth is a great warrior who is used to making life-and-death decisions in battle, but here he is torn about the murder. Eventually he decides to do it. Maybe this is because he really is an evil man. Maybe he is so mixed up that he cannot sort out the difference between right and wrong. Perhaps he is under the power of the witches. Maybe he does not really know what to do and is acting on the spur of the moment, without really thinking too much. Whatever the reason, he has reached the point of no return.

Scene 2

> **❝Had he not resembled My father as he slept, I had done't❞**

It is night-time. Lady Macbeth waits anxiously for Macbeth as he murders Duncan. Until now, Lady Macbeth has seemed very determined and strong. Here she is very much <u>on edge</u>. Although earlier she seemed able to do the most terrible deeds, now she reveals a more sensitive side when she says that she could not

Text commentary

Explore

This scene is rich in stagecraft and the noises and props play key roles. How would you present this scene to give the maximum effect to these additional elements?

carry out the murder herself because the sleeping Duncan reminded her of her father. This is the first sign of Lady Macbeth's conscience and feelings of guilt. She, too, seems to realise the wrongness of the murder.

> ❝ *Macbeth does murder sleep,*
> *the innocent sleep* ❞

Macbeth enters and says he has killed Duncan as he slept. Sleep represents innocence and peace, and Macbeth imagines he has also murdered these.

Duncan's innocent servants can say 'Amen' in their prayers, but Macbeth cannot, which is a firm indication of the evilness of his crime. This is not simply an ordinary killing, but the murder of a man **chosen** **by** **God** to rule. He is terrified because he knows that he can never be forgiven for his crime. Lady Macbeth says these worries are 'brain-sickly'.

Lady Macbeth has been the organiser of the murder from the outset and here, once she has again **taken** **charge** of herself, she clears up after Macbeth's bunglings. She 'drugged the possets' of the grooms sleeping in the outer chamber; she laid the daggers ready; all Macbeth had to do was the deed itself. Now, here he is with two blood-stained daggers which should have been left with the grooms, the supposed murderers.

Explore

Pontius Pilot was the Roman senator responsible for decreeing the crucifixion of Christ. He symbolically rinsed his hands to illustrate that he would have nothing more to do with Christ's martyrdom. Why might this be a significant religious detail?

The terrified Macbeth is incapable of returning to the murder scene, so Lady Macbeth does so, smearing the grooms with blood. On her return she finds Macbeth transfixed with thoughts of blood and guilt and once again takes charge of the situation. She tells Macbeth to go and wash the blood from his hands. She means the **visible** **blood** on his hands, but Macbeth fears for his **blood-stained** **soul**. The two images of blood and water are again combined, as in Act 1, Scene 1, but here they

Text commentary

are presented in a much more horrific way. The blood in Act 1 was proof of a valiant battle, here it is proof of guilt and treason.

Sleep is described here as 'chief nourisher in life's feast'. Sleep and food are seen as essential parts of nature. Both are needed for life. Macbeth has **destroyed** **this** **natural** **order** and this is seen again later, when he destroys the calm and order of his own coronation banquet.

> *These deeds must not be thought*
> *After these ways; so it will make us mad*

Shakespeare conveys Macbeth's feelings of guilt not only in what he says, but in how he says it. Most striking in this scene is that his speeches keep turning in on themselves, constantly returning to a word or a phrase. 'Amen', for instance ('So be it', the traditional end of a prayer), is never out of his thoughts, though he cannot say it and mean it. Lady Macbeth realises that they must not dwell on their actions, or they will go insane, and in a precursor to her later demise, there are many references to insanity: 'mad', 'hurt minds' and 'brain-sickly'.

> *Will all great Neptune's ocean wash this blood*
> *Clean from my hand?*

To complete the deed, Lady Macbeth takes the daggers from her husband and places them near the drunken grooms. She chastises him for his cowardice and makes many references to blood: 'bleed', 'painted', 'gild', 'colour', 'red'. We are made to realise the significance of the spilled blood, and it is an image which will now seep into virtually every scene of the play.

Scene 3

The castle's Porter (night watchman) answers the knocking at the gate. Macduff has come to wake the king, but discovers his dead

Explore

Notice how Shakespeare uses language differently for the Porter. His words do not have the chant-like rhythm of the witches, nor the poetic sound of Macbeth's soliloquies. Why might a prose style have been chosen for this character?

body instead. During the panic and confusion that results, Duncan's sons decide to escape to safety.

The comical Porter adds nothing to the plot, but this is not his purpose. Dramatically, shorter scenes in the play are either a reminder of what has happened so far or a preparation for what is coming. This scene is deliberately light-hearted and **relieves the tension** of the last scene, as well as contrasting with the next, when Duncan's murder is discovered.

The Porter imagines he is the gatekeeper in Hell. This was a traditional figure in plays before Shakespeare's time, but it has a special importance here. Macbeth's castle has, in a way, become the gateway to Hell. The Porter makes jokes about the perils of drink and about having too much of a good thing; about a farmer who is ruined because of his ambition; about people who destroy themselves because they confuse truth with half-truths (they 'equivocate' between the truth and lies); and about a tailor who was hanged for stealing precious fabric. The Porter's **jokes** are cleverly designed to **tell us something about Macbeth**, who you might feel is also confused; he too has become intoxicated with evil, will be ruined by having too much ambition, believes too much in the witches' half-truths and he has 'stolen' the king's crown. Certainly the Porter gives a **satirical picture of a dishonest world**.

The Porter also serves an additional dramatic purpose. During Shakespeare's time, characters such as these were almost like stand-up comedians. The actors would have been allowed to improvise some of their lines, making subtle and sly references and jokes about topical events.

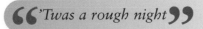
❝_'Twas a rough night_**❞**

Macduff and Lennox have come to wake the king. They describe the storm during the night. The description of the **storm** **is** **symbolic** of the effect that Duncan's murder is already having on the natural balance of the world. It also reminds us of the power of the witches, who arrive in thunderous weather and have the power to command storms. The murder of the king has filled the night with screams of death and other portents. Sickness and evil seem to have infected even the earth itself when Lennox says that he has heard that the earth 'was feverous and did shake'. Macbeth agrees, using dramatic irony, that "twas a rough night'.

Explore

How should the actor playing Macbeth say "twas a rough night'? Would he be visibly shaken or would the evilness of his deed make him say this line in a much more sinister way?

❝O horror, horror, horror❞

The imagery which Macduff uses when he tells the others that he has found Duncan murdered is significant. The murder has unleashed **chaos** on the world and is **sacrilegious** (against God). Macduff says that to look at the murdered body will 'destroy your sight with a new Gorgon'. The Gorgons were three sisters in Greek mythology with snakes for hair, who were so hideous that the sight of them turned people to stone. How do these creatures fit with the other female characters in the play so far?

Macduff describes sleep as an imitation ('counterfeit') of death and tells Banquo to rise up like a 'sprite' (a ghost) from its 'grave' (his bed) to look at 'this horror'. Later in the play, Banquo does actually arise as a ghost from his grave to visit another 'horror' when he returns to haunt Macbeth.

Showing his 'false face', Macbeth pretends that life now has no meaning for him. Images of blood and water appear again: '**the spring, the head, the fountain of your blood / Is stopped**'. Macbeth praises the king in **over-the-top**, rich language, referring to precious metals, 'silver skin' and 'golden blood'. Echoing Lady Macbeth's pun on gild, meaning gold and guilt (Act 2, Scene 2, lines 58–59), he combines imagery of jewels with references to blood and wounds: 'gore', 'steeped', 'colours', 'gashed'.

Lennox says it appears that Duncan's guards are guilty of the murder. Macbeth says he was so angry when he saw Duncan's body that he killed them. This is a tricky moment for Macbeth. The others would have wanted to question the guards. Macduff wonders why Macbeth should have destroyed the only way of finding out. Of course, Macbeth knows that the guards would have denied the murder because they were innocent. There was a risk that they might have been believed.

Lady Macbeth faints **just** **at** **the** **right** **moment**, but it may be too late to save Macbeth from suspicion. This killing of the grooms is also the first sign that Macbeth is about to go his own way; this was not part of the plan! Interestingly, Lady Macbeth remains **silent** for much of this scene, leaving Macbeth to deal with the many questions. It is also intriguing that although Macbeth's actions are suspicious, no one thinks to question him, not even Banquo, who simply declares his allegiance to God and vows 'Against the undivulged pretence I fight / Of treasonous malice' – a clear warning to the treacherous Macbeth.

Explore

Is Lady Macbeth's faint genuine? What reasons could she have for faking such an act?

❝There's daggers in men's smiles❞

Explore

This is a confusing scene, with multiple entrances and exits, exclamations, rhetorical devices, different conversations, sound effects and stage directions. How would you manage to stage such a busy scene to best effect?

Duncan's sons, **Malcolm** **and** **Donalbain**, decide to escape in case they too are targets to be murdered next. Donalbain does not appear again in the play but he leaves with a **telling** **remark** about how there are 'daggers in men's smiles' all around them. This echoes the 'fair is foul' theme of the play and shows a level of **perception** on his part. It makes us wonder if he has seen through Macbeth's act. Certainly, it would be hard for Macbeth to maintain the impression that he is a 'flower', having just admitted to a frenzied killing of two sleeping guards. His true serpent nature is not being very well hidden.

Scene 4

66 *Hours dreadful and things strange* **99**

Ross, Macduff and the Old Man discuss the current situation. This is another scene, like the one with the Porter, where the audience gets the chance to digest what has happened so far. Stress is laid on the **unnaturalness** of the murder and how its evil root has begun to **poison** all nature. Darkness 'strangles' the daylight, a falcon is killed by an owl, and Duncan's horses have turned wild and eaten each other.

66 *The sovereignty will fall upon Macbeth* **99**

In answer to questions, Macduff says that because Malcolm and Donalbain have fled, they are suspected of having paid the guards to do the murder. Ross mentions another one of the main themes in the play when he comments that people's '**thriftless ambition**' will foolishly destroy and consume the very thing on which their life and future depend. Meanwhile, Macbeth has hurried off to be crowned.

Extending the clothing motif, Macduff hopes that the country's 'old robes' (King Duncan) do not turn out to 'sit easier' (be more comfortable) than 'the new' (King Macbeth). It is significant that Macduff is staying away from the coronation at Scone: he does not trust Macbeth, he will not be part of his court, but for the moment he will not speak out.

Who? What? Where? When? Why? How?

1   Who is on night watch at the castle as the Act opens?

2   Who says he does not want to sleep, though tired, and why?

3   What happened during the night, according to Lennox, Ross and the Old Man?

4   What vision does Macbeth see and how does he interpret it?

5   Where do Malcolm and Donalbain escape to?

6   Where is Macbeth invested (crowned) as king, and who is notably absent?

7   Why did Macbeth kill Duncan's guards? Why does he say he did so, and how does he get out of having to explain more fully?

8   Why can Lady Macbeth not kill Duncan herself?

9   How do the sounds of a bell and knocking connect in Macbeth's mind with Duncan's death?

10   How do the Porter's anecdotes reflect on the action of the play?

Open quotes

Find the line – and complete the phrase or sentence.

1   'Or art thou but a dagger of the mind…'

2   'But wherefore could not I pronounce 'Amen'?…'

3   'Will all great Neptune's ocean…'

4   'There's nothing serious in mortality…'

5   'Tis unnatural…'

Night moves

This Act is full of actions and images to do with sleeping, waking and wakefulness. Find three lines in the text on each of the following themes.

1   sleep and death

2   sleeplessness

3   waking and summoning from sleep

4   dreams and nightmares

Text commentary

Act 3

Scene 1

> **❝I fear / Thou played'st most foully for it❞**

Time has passed and Macbeth is now king. In this short soliloquy, Banquo tells the audience that he **suspects** that Macbeth became king by foul means. He also dwells on the witches' message for himself. Banquo does not suggest to the audience that he feels that he is in any danger from Macbeth and he remains **loyal** to him.

> **❝If he had been forgotton
> It had been a gap in our great feast❞**

Macbeth invites Banquo to the banquet even though he is about to arrange for Banquo to be murdered (so obviously does not expect to see him there). Lady Macbeth, now queen, is overly flattering to Banquo and tells him that without him there would be a space at the table. This is deeply ironic because even when Banquo is dead there is still no empty chair, as Macbeth discovers! Notice how Macbeth is very keen to find out if Banquo's son Fleance is going riding with his father. Macbeth is **afraid** **of** **Banquo** because he knows too much about the meetings with the witches. He is **afraid** **of** **Fleance** because Banquo's descendants are to become kings.

Notice how Macbeth has counted on the predictions of the witches coming true up to this point. Now he wants to prevent their prediction about Banquo also coming true.

"A borrower of the night"

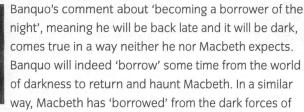

Banquo's comment about 'becoming a borrower of the night', meaning he will be back late and it will be dark, comes true in a way neither he nor Macbeth expects. Banquo will indeed 'borrow' some time from the world of darkness to return and haunt Macbeth. In a similar way, Macbeth has 'borrowed' from the dark forces of chaos, except that in his case he will have to repay the debt with his life.

"Our fears in Banquo stick deep"

In a soliloquy, Macbeth tells the audience why he is afraid of Banquo. He says that Banquo is brave, clever and wise and that he is the only man he fears. Banquo was not afraid to talk to the witches and demanded that they tell him what the future had in store for them. Macbeth sees his time on the throne as **fruitless** because Banquo's children will be the future kings.

Explore

How do the words of this speech remind us of Lady Macbeth's views on children?

Macbeth's '**seeds**' will not grow but Banquo's will. This is a reminder that King Duncan promised to make Macbeth '**full of growing**'. The speech is filled with images of **children and fertility** – 'father', 'line', 'fruitless', 'barren', 'unlineal', 'son', 'issue' and 'seeds' – and contrasts the idea of Banquo's descendants with Macbeth's lack of offspring.

Macbeth thinks that he has corrupted himself and murdered Duncan for Banquo's benefit. He has not done what he has done just for somebody else to get the rewards. Macbeth's battle with fate begins as he decides to deliberately prevent Banquo's heirs from becoming kings.

"I will put that business in your bosoms"

Text commentary

Macbeth has **recruited** **murderers** to kill Banquo. You might wonder why he does not do it himself – after all, he is a great warrior who is used to killing. Perhaps the answer lies in his reaction to killing King Duncan. Or it might be that he does not want to risk detection. Maybe the reasons that Macbeth gives are actually the true ones.

Like Macbeth in Act 1, the murderers are men driven by circumstances to turn criminal. They are not professional killers; they have both fallen on hard times. They previously thought that Macbeth ('our innocent self') was to blame for their hardship, but he has explained that their enemy was really Banquo. In order to maintain the **dramatic** **pace** in this scene, Shakespeare has Macbeth refer to a previous meeting with the hired killers. This maintains the **momentum**, but also suggests that Macbeth is being **hasty**. He is spending much less time deliberating over this next murder.

Scene 2

Lady Macbeth is very **uneasy**. Her **anxiety** is made worse because Macbeth is keeping himself to himself instead of being with her. She tries to encourage her husband to forget the past, saying that '**what's** **done** **is** **done**', but she is clearly troubled by what has happened. Perhaps she is not a **monster** after all, simply a **wife** trying to protect, encourage and support her husband.

> ❝*O full of scorpions is my mind*❞

Macbeth says he is afflicted by **terrible** **dreams**, developing the sleep image. He seems almost to envy the dead King Duncan who, he says, 'sleeps well'. Although Duncan is dead, Macbeth says, at least nothing can hurt him any more. Sleep is an important theme in the play, because in Shakespeare's time it was believed that the **good** **and**

Explore

There are many references to sleep in the play. Can you find other examples?

pure of heart found **untroubled sleep**, while those with **evil natures** could not rest and were plagued by **nightmares**. See how this idea is developed in Act 5, Scene 1.

Explore

Why doesn't Macbeth tell his wife about his plans? Is it to protect her, or do you think he has other reasons?

Macbeth's sleep is becoming tormented: 'O, full of scorpions is my mind'. This is an important metaphor and suggests that his thoughts are being tainted by **venomous** plans. He says that as darkness falls, 'there shall be done a deed of dreadful note' – but he won't tell Lady Macbeth what it is: '**Be innocent of the knowledge, dearest chuck**.'

Macbeth's final words in this scene are ominous and say a lot about how his mind is working. He says that **wickedness grows stronger through more wickedness**, and he uses the theme of darkness and witchcraft to illustrate his evil intentions: 'seeling night', 'rooky wood', 'crow' and 'night's black agents'. It seems that Macbeth is now committed to the path of evil. Later, Macbeth will say that he has gone so far along the path of evil that it is as easy for him to go on as to turn back.

Scene 3

Explore

Who do you think this third killer might be? Could it be one of the other characters in the play?

Darkness falls and a third murderer arrives to join the other two. Macbeth seems to trust no one. The identity of the **Third Murderer** is open to question ('the perfect spy o' the time' referred to in Scene 1, perhaps), but you should note how he takes charge, identifying victims and assessing what is happening.

This scene is also full of references to darkness overpowering light, which is a metaphor for evil overcoming goodness. Just before the murder, '**the west yet glimmers with some streaks of day**'. Banquo and Fleance arrive with a **burning torch**. One of the murderers asks who struck out the light, which has two meanings. The comment is echoed in Macbeth's later words about his wife, 'Out, out, brief candle'.

The murder of Banquo strikes out the last glimmer of light and hope for Macbeth's soul, but the escape of Fleance allows the witches' predictions to come true. Although 'lesser' in power than Macbeth, he is also 'greater' than him in terms of **goodness** **and** **future** **power**. Banquo's descendants will indeed become kings in spite of all Macbeth's efforts to prevent this.

Scene 4

❝ *Play the humble host* ❞

The guests arrive at Macbeth's celebration banquet and are asked to take their places. At first, things seem civil and organised. Then the murderer arrives to give Macbeth the news that Banquo is dead, but that Fleance has escaped.

Macbeth has already imagined a dagger, now he believes he sees Banquo's **ghost**. Again, Lady Macbeth takes command, quietly accusing her husband of being a coward as she did at the time of Duncan's murder, but she apologises to the guests and covers up for him.

Explore

Do you think, like the dagger, that this vision is real, or is it simply a sign of Macbeth's evil nature and his guilty conscience? Or is he really sick?

Macbeth throws the calm and organised atmosphere of the **banquet** into turmoil in the same way as his reign as king will throw **Scotland** into chaos. Macbeth was probably hoping for a dignified occasion to mark his crowning, but has ended up with confusion. This is an ominous portent of the way things are generally going for Macbeth.

"*never shake / Thy gory locks at me!*"

Explore

If you were the director, how would you direct this scene? What advice would you give to the actors playing Macbeth, Lady Macbeth and the startled guests about the delivery of their lines?

Macbeth fears Banquo's ghost because it has come to accuse him of its murder. In the previous scene Macbeth stated how lucky Duncan was because he was **at peace in death**. Here, the dead **rise up** again, and so Macbeth worries that even in death there may be no peace for himself. Lady Macbeth says that all he needs is **sleep**, but this is ironic as Macbeth '**has murdered sleep**' and Banquo has risen from his 'sleep'. Remember the further irony that Macbeth asked Banquo to 'fail not our feast'.

In a sense, **Macbeth summons Banquo's ghost**: each time he sees the vision, he has just mentioned Banquo and how he misses his presence. Notice that Banquo **takes the king's chair**, in much the same way that Macbeth stole it originally from Duncan.

"*Blood will have blood*"

After the ghost leaves and the guests have gone it is almost dawn. Night, says Lady Macbeth, is 'almost at odds with morning'. She cannot tell whether it is night or day. In their world, because they have overturned the natural order, King and Queen Macbeth do not know darkness from light or evil from good. Fair has become foul and foul has become fair.

Sounding like a true tyrant, Macbeth talks about wading in blood, an image which echoes the Captain's speech about 'bathing in blood' at the start of the play. Macbeth feels that his journey into a sea of blood has gone so far that he may as well hold his course now. Macbeth does not allow himself the option of turning back, even though he has already changed fate by electing to murder first Duncan and now Banquo.

Text commentary

Scene 5

❝*riddles and affairs of death*❞

Explore

Can you find any evidence in the characterisation or style of the language which might suggest that this was written by someone other than Shakespeare?

Hecate scolds the other witches for not including her in their dealings with Macbeth, and says she will be with them next time they meet him. Many commentators think that this short scene was not written by Shakespeare but was added later by a lesser playwright, and some versions of the play leave it out.

Scene 6

**❝*Our suffering country*
Under a hand accursed❞**

Lennox and another Lord discuss the terrible state of Scotland under Macbeth's rule, and hope that the King of England will help them. Lennox's initial speech is presumably ironic. He determinedly praises Macbeth, reiterates Macbeth's version of the events on the night of Duncan's murder and talks about the new king's 'noble' actions. However, in a following line he refers to Macbeth as the 'tyrant'. He **echoes strong themes in the play** by longing for better, ordered times when food cupboards are well stocked, nights are for sleeping and when banquets do not contain 'bloody knives'. More importantly, they desperately need a good king. The first mention of English assistance comes in the news that Macduff is to plead with the English king and Siward to help restore peace in Scotland.

This scene is another example of minor characters describing events so far. This **helps the audience keep up to date** with events that have happened or are happening somewhere else; and reminds them of the important ideas in the play.

Who? What? Where? When? Why? How?

1   Who is charged to 'fail not our feast', and why is this ironic?

2   What empty signs of kingship have been given to Macbeth if Banquo's son lives?

3   What is life in Scotland like under Macbeth's kingship?

4   Where is Macduff and what is he doing? Where should he be?

5   Where is everyone when Banquo is attacked?

6   Why does Macbeth not sit down when invited to do so by Ross at the feast?

7   Why does Macbeth envy Duncan?

8   How does Macbeth justify the attack on Banquo, to himself and to the murderers?

9   How does Banquo deal with the witches' prophecy?

Open quotes

Find the line – and complete the phrase or sentence.

1   'Thou hast it now…'

2   'To be thus is nothing…'

3   'Naught's had, all's spent…'

4   'I am in blood / Stepped in so far…'

5   'Better be with the dead…'

Creature features?

The use of animal imagery continues in this Act.

1   What dark creatures are mentioned in Scene 2 by Macbeth?

2   Who is the 'worm' that 'Hath nature that in time will venom breed, / No teeth for the present'?

3   What exotic, ferocious beasts does Macbeth dare the spirit to manifest rather than Banquo's likeness?

Text commentary

Act 4

Scene 1

❝*Double double, toil and trouble*❞

Disgusting objects are thrown into a steaming pot as the witches concoct a charm. The dismembered bits of animals and humans are <u>symbols</u> <u>of</u> <u>the</u> <u>witches'</u> <u>destructive</u> <u>behaviour</u> in the play. Throughout this speech the witches talk in <u>rhyme</u>, which makes everything they say sound like a magic spell being chanted.

Explore

Why are some of these gruesome ingredients so appropriate? Do any of the creatures mentioned have any significance according to superstition or religion?

The witches' 'gruel' is also an image of formless confusion, the <u>primaeval</u> <u>chaos</u> into which the powers of evil are constantly striving to plunge creation. This reflects the Elizabethans' belief about the nature of the world and the relationship between good and evil, order and disorder.

**❝*By the pricking of my thumbs*
Something wicked this way comes❞**

The witches indicate that Macbeth is wicked like themselves. In contrast to Act 1, Scene 3, Macbeth now talks to them in an almost <u>conspiratorial,</u> <u>conversational</u> way. He does not seem afraid as he was at first. Macbeth doesn't care how much damage or chaos he causes, he just wants to know the future, and <u>demands</u> that the witches show it to him. Macbeth seems to have **dismissed Banquo's warning** that the witches will use Macbeth's readiness to believe their predictions as a way of destroying him. Macbeth has conveniently forgotton that words can be twisted and that appearances can be very deceptive.

> ❝*Macbeth, Macbeth, Macbeth:*
> *beware Macduff*❞

Macbeth is shown three apparitions and a vision of the future. The first apparition is of a **decapitated head wearing armour**. It knows Macbeth's thoughts and tells him to beware of Macduff. Although Macbeth probably thinks that the head is a vision of Macduff, you will see by the end of the play that it might also be Macbeth's head that has been cut off.

> ❝*None of woman born*
> *Shall harm Macbeth*❞

The second apparition is of a child **covered in blood**. It tells Macbeth that he cannot be killed by anyone 'born of woman'. There are various candidates for the 'bloody child': Fleance has just escaped a bloody ambush, Macduff's children are about to die at Macbeth's bidding and Lady Macbeth talks of slaying an innocent baby. However, given the message he later imparts, the most telling identification is with Macduff who, unknown to Macbeth, was 'from his mother's womb untimely ripped'.

> ❝*Macbeth shall never vanquished be until*
> *Great Birnam Wood to high Dunsinane hill*
> *Shall come against him*❞

This third apparition is of a **child wearing a crown and holding a branch**. This could represent Malcolm, who later on in the play orders his army to conceal its size by hiding behind branches from Birnam Wood. It also gives the audience a visual reminder of

Explore

In superstition, three is a powerful number. How many lists of three can you find in the play?

Macbeth's family tree, which is barren, and indicates that Macbeth has even tampered with the natural world. It is significant that two of the three apparitions are children. Macbeth has been afraid of children all through the play, because of what they may grow into. He is also desperate to be reassured about his future. Remember Hecate's words: 'And you all know, security / Is mortal's chiefest enemy.'

❝will the line stretch out to th' crack of doom?❞

When the witches show Macbeth a fourth vision, his worst fears are realised – his hold on the crown will only be temporary. He finds it painful to look at what the witches show him. He sees a row of kings stretching out before him with Banquo smiling and pointing at them to show that they are his descendants.

The ball and sceptre that the kings hold are symbols of the future joining together of England and Scotland. What Macbeth sees in the glass (a crystal ball) is **King James I and his line of ancestors**. Since James I was king when Shakespeare wrote the play and was known to have a deep interest in witches and the supernatural, the play would have been a favourite of his. The first performance is supposed to have been at King James I's court.

Explore

How does Macbeth take the witches' news? What do you think it will prompt him to do?

The witches mock Macbeth with words, but they know how shocked he is and pretend to cheer him up with music and dancing. Then they vanish forever from the play. The prophecies resemble those of the ancient oracles, which never told lies but often deceived.

❝Macduff is fled to England❞

News arrives that Macduff has fled and Macbeth is once again the **man of action**. Without hesitation, he commands that Macduff's castle is to be attacked and everyone in it murdered. He is now ruthless and __decisive__ and has __no time__ for the kind of soul-searching he engaged in earlier in the play. Neither does he even consider sharing his plans with his wife, who now seems to have taken a more subservient role. His character is very much that of a __ruthless dictator__ who knows no moral quandary.

Scene 2

Lady Macduff is fearful and outraged that her husband has left his family. Ross reassures her that Macduff is merely being wise, and says that the times are __uncertain__. His short speech stresses the deep __suspicion__ that now runs through the land ruled by Macbeth. He says that __people are afraid__, like those who 'float upon a wild and violent sea', and that men are now traitors and __do not know themselves__. In both of his comments you should be able to see references to some of the main themes in the play, as well as to Macbeth's current state.

❝ *Young fry of treachery!* ❞

Explore

Lady Macduff only features in one scene, but she has an important role in the play. Why do you think Shakespeare chose to add this character, and with whom does she contrast?

After Ross has gone, Lady Macduff talks to her son about his father's absence. Their conversation is full of light-hearted jokes but is serious underneath. They talk about traitors and whether Macduff is one, but ironically the boy humorously makes the point that there are __more traitors than honest men__. Lady Macduff has no ambition and is not interested in power.

A messenger arrives to warn Lady Macduff to run away because danger approaches. She says that although she has done no harm, she knows that doing harm is sometimes applauded while doing good is sometimes dangerous. This echoes the witches' first appearance and emphasises the way in which fair is foul and foul is fair under Macbeth's rule. The murderers appear and begin to carry out Macbeth's orders.

 Lady Macduff's death and that of her son are important in the play because they are examples of the tyranny and evil of Macbeth. The vulnerability and age of the babies is emphasised by descriptions such as 'little ones', 'fry' (meaning baby fish) and 'egg'. Unlike the previous murders, these deaths serve **no purpose**. They represent **brutality for its own sake** and mark the lowest point in Macbeth's moral decline. The deaths also indicate an important turning-point in the action of the play. Macduff was already convinced that Macbeth was a cruel tyrant who should be toppled from the throne, but his personal grief sets him on the path of revenge that gives him added determination to kill Macbeth.

Scene 3

> **❝Angels are bright still, though the brightest fell❞**

Explore

This is a unique scene in the play. It is the only one set in England, away from the action and away from Macbeth. What dramatic purposes does this scene serve?

This important scene reintroduces Malcolm and shows how mistrust and suspicion have grown between people under Macbeth's rule. The scene opens with Macduff telling Malcolm how every morning there are new widows in Scotland.

Malcolm seems worried and suspicious of Macduff. Of course, Macduff was once loyal to Macbeth, he was one of those in the castle the night Duncan was murdered, he has not yet been harmed by Macbeth, and he has left his family behind in Scotland. Malcolm comments that even the devil started life as an angel in Heaven. Neither man yet knows about the murder of Macduff's family.

> **❝It weeps, it bleeds, and each new day a gash❞**

Malcolm talks about the state of Scotland, using blood imagery to compare the land to an open wound, like a cut earned in battle. The image also suggests that Macbeth's actions are literally bleeding the country dry.

Explore

Personification is a technique where an inanimate object, like the land of Scotland, is given human qualities. Can you find other examples in the play? What effect is created here?

Explore

What noble qualities does Malcolm list and how many does Macbeth possess? Has Macbeth changed from the beginning of the play?

In a long conversation with Macduff, Malcolm tests his loyalty by pretending to be more wicked and cruel than Macbeth. Many of the crimes he says he would commit are things which Macbeth has already done to Scotland. Malcolm lists the qualities that kings should have.

By the end of this conversation Malcolm is sure of Macduff's loyalty. <u>Loyalty</u> is an important idea in the play, but unthinking loyalty to the king is not enough. Sometimes the king is a man like Macbeth. Loyalty was supposed to be to the <u>state</u> and to the idea of <u>order</u>, not just to the individual who happened to be king. This view was very important to the people of Shakespeare's time, which is why it plays such a big part in the story of *Macbeth*. It was important for Shakespeare to establish that Malcolm will be a good king and that his is a crusade for the <u>powers of goodness and justice</u> against the evil tyrant that Macbeth has become.

❝❝*He hath a heavenly gift of prophecy*❞❞

The English Doctor tells Malcolm and Macduff about the King of England and how noble and good he is. He says that the king is so holy that just by touching the sick he can cure them because he has a '<u>heavenly gift of prophecy</u>'. Shakespeare's audience would have considered this as the opposite of the witches' powers, although it may sound like a parallel to us.

These superstitions were questioned even in Shakespeare's day, but they are used here to reinforce the idea that the rightful king was <u>appointed by God</u> and was a <u>force for good</u>, supported by the powers of heaven. Contrast the English king's healing powers with the way Macbeth cannot cure himself of his suffering. Later on, the Scottish Doctor cannot cure Lady Macbeth of her illness because it, too, is a sickness of the mind.

❝ *Be this the whetstone of your sword* ❞

Acting again as a messenger in the play, Ross arrives with the latest bad news from Scotland. He reluctantly tells Macduff about his murdered family. Macduff swears **revenge**, which in those days was thought to be a **proper** and **manly** feeling. Even Malcolm encourages Macduff to use his anger and grief to sharpen the blade of his sword, so he can kill the wrongful king.

At the start of the play, King Duncan said he would 'plant' Macbeth. Banquo asked the witches to look into the 'seeds of time' and say which ones would grow and which would not. The idea that all things have a **natural** **cycle** or season is repeated here. Malcolm describes himself as the **angel of death** or a deadly harvester, with Macbeth as a fruit '**ripe for shaking**' that will soon fall.

Who? What? Where? When? Why? How?

1 Who is 'bloody, luxurious, avaricious, false, deceitful, / Sudden, malicious'?

2 Who is with Lady Macduff just before she is attacked?

3 What gifts is Edward said to possess?

4 What is Malcolm's plan when Macduff arrives?

5 Where does Macbeth meet the witches this time?

6 Why, does Malcolm imply, might Macduff still be loyal to Macbeth?

7 Why, according to Malcolm, should Macduff be generally hopeful?

8 How does Macbeth resolve to 'make assurance double sure', and why is this ironic?

Open quotes

Find the line – and complete the phrase or sentence.

1 'Be bloody, bold and resolute:...'

2 'No boasting like a fool...'

3 'Angels are bright still...'

4 'Each new morn...'

5 'Macbeth is ripe for shaking...'

A matter of trust

Trust and loyalty have also become a major issue in the play by this time. Two major incidents in this Act outline the theme.

1 List the three apparitions shown to Macbeth: why are they ambiguous or 'equivocal'?

2 Who says of the witches: 'damn'd all those that trust them!', and why is this ironic?

3 Who implies that Macduff is a traitor, and why?

4 Who is a 'child of integrity'?

5 Why is Macduff confused by Malcolm's confession, and whose situation does this echo?

Text commentary

Act 5

Scene 1

Until now, Lady Macbeth has not seemed bothered by bad dreams. Now she spends her nights wandering about – literally a lost soul – and insists that a light is on continually because she is afraid of the darkness (perhaps in more senses than one). The doctor says that Lady Macbeth's eyes are open, but the gentlewoman says that '<u>their</u> <u>senses</u> <u>are</u> <u>shut</u>', meaning that she is unconscious.

❝*Out damned spot!*❞

In her waking nightmare, Lady Macbeth cannot wash spots of blood from her hands. Compare this with her behaviour following Duncan's murder, when she counselled Macbeth that a little water would <u>wipe</u> <u>away</u> <u>all</u> <u>trace</u> <u>of</u> <u>the</u> <u>murder</u>. At the time the play was written, people thought that witches carried the Devil's mark on their bodies somewhere, so the 'spot' could be a metaphor for this. In what other ways has Lady Macbeth been linked with the witches and dark forces?

Explore

Look closely at Lady Macbeth's language. How have her speech patterns changed?

Lady Macbeth's speeches allow the audience an insight into her mental state. She is a very different character now from the one we first met. By contrast, in this Act Macbeth becomes more like the decisive man of action from the play's opening.

Scene 2

In this scene and the following three short scenes, the action moves quickly from place to place towards the climax. In addition, several of the main themes in the play appear in rapid succession.

The Scottish Lords begin to gather their army against Macbeth. Angus says that Macbeth's title of king now hangs '<u>loose about him like a giant's robe upon a dwarfish thief</u>' (clothing). Caithness says that Macbeth's cause is '<u>distempered</u>', meaning weak or diseased, because it is not properly tempered or hardened (chaos). He also talks about their army as medicine for the diseased country – '<u>sickly weal</u>'. Lennox says the bloodletting – 'purge' – that is coming is needed to '<u>drown the weeds</u>' (nature and return to order).

Scene 3

I am sick at heart

Macbeth is told that the English army is approaching his castle. He tries to reassure himself that everything could still turn out for the best, although he knows that this is really a false hope. In a short soliloquy, he admits that by his actions he has denied himself all the good things that should come with old age, such as love, honour and friends. In spite of all the evil deeds he has done, because of Shakespeare's skilful work here it is possible for the audience to feel sorry for Macbeth.

Explore

How does Shakespeare use language and imagery to provoke pity for Macbeth in this scene?

Notice Macbeth's use of imagery about withering plants and the suggestion that his own growing season is ended. He seems to know that the time for his end has come. Having accepted this, he calls for his armour. In some productions,

Seyton's name is pronounced 'Satan'. Do you think Shakespeare deliberately included this possibility? If so, what might he be trying to suggest? Something of the warrior we first knew is reappearing, as Macbeth says he will fight until his flesh is hacked from his bones.

The doctor tells Macbeth that his wife must cure herself, because she is suffering from a troubled mind rather than a physical illness. Macbeth's anger at this could well be because he knows that both he and his wife are now beyond the help of this world. Only their deaths will 'cure' them.

Scene 4

"*Let every soldier hew him down a bough*"

All the nobles from earlier in the play have come together at Birnam Wood to join Malcolm's army. Their calm and determined mood contrasts with Macbeth's bouts of fury and shouting. Malcolm's clever strategy (they cut branches to hide their number from Macbeth's forces) allows the audience to suddenly understand how the witches may have duped Macbeth, and how easily the meaning of their predictions could be twisted into falsehood.

Scene 5

"*Out, out, brief candle*"

Macbeth says that once he would have been frightened by a shriek in the night. This is a reminder of the owl-cry heard at Duncan's murder. Now, Macbeth feels he can no longer be frightened because he has seen so many horrors. At once, and ironically, he is startled by a cry.

Explore

'All the world's a stage'. Macbeth's words echo those spoken by Jacques in *As You Like It*. Look up this soliloquy and compare its sentiments with those spoken by Macbeth.

Macbeth seems numb at the news of his wife's death. He talks about the **pointlessness of life**, which ends only in 'dusty death'. It is significant that he compares Lady Macbeth's life to a **flickering candle**, easily and suddenly snuffed out – particularly as, in her last few months, she was terrified of the dark. He realises that all his efforts have been fruitless. Using one of Shakespeare's favourite images, he compares life to a **passing show**, a **shadow**, a fleeting thing. He says life is as meaningless as the sound and fury of an idiot's tale, performed on the stage, but with no real substance or truth.

> ❝*Blow wind, come wrack;*
> *At least we'll die with harness on our back*❞

Explore

Who do you think is more responsible for Macbeth's situation – himself or the witches?

The witches did not lie to Macbeth, but their predictions have come true in a way that he could not have foreseen. It looks as if the wood is moving towards Macbeth's castle.

Macbeth is weary of life, but vows to die a warrior. Throughout the play, Macbeth is associated with drums, bells, alarms, storms, lightning, the screeching of wild animals and other sudden loud noises. Calling now upon the '**sound and fury**' of alarm bells, storms and shipwrecks, Macbeth goes out to do **battle**. It is visually important that he chooses to dress himself again in the vestments of a **soldier**. Macbeth feels safest dressed as a warrior.

Scenes 6, 7 and 8

Explore

Bear-baiting was one of the Elizabethans' favourite pastimes. Research others and see if you can find references to them in this play.

> ❝*Bear-like I must fight the course*❞

The attacking army arrives at the castle. Macbeth takes comfort in the only prediction of the witches that has not yet turned against him – no man born of woman can harm him. Using an animal simile, he compares himself to a bear, tied up and over-powered, but angry and strong to the end.

" I bear a charmed life "

Macbeth kills Young Siward, emphasising his savage nature, but the castle is conquered. Macbeth is then confronted by Macduff, but is reluctant to fight him because of what he has already done to Macduff's family. Macbeth learns that Macduff was taken from his mother's womb early (probably a Caesarean birth): 'untimely ripp'd'. Macbeth sees that he has again been tricked by the witches and refuses to fight. Macduff says that, in that case, he will be tethered and put on show like a rare monster. This is too much for Macbeth, who has **personal pride and honour** and could not bear his life to end this way. He hurls himself at Macduff. He is killed and his severed head is put on display for all to see.

" Invite to see us crowned at Scone "

At the start of the play the first Thane of Cawdor died bravely, and Malcolm said that 'nothing in his life became him like the leaving it'. You should think about whether this was also true of Macbeth (the second Thane of Cawdor). Did he die more nobly than he lived? The final speech in the play comes from Malcolm, the new king, who announces that he will reward the nobles who have helped him. The imagery of planting and growing appears again. His final judgement is that Macbeth was a 'butcher' and Lady Macbeth his 'fiend-like queen'. You should look back though the play and come to your own verdict.

Who? What? Where? When? Why? How?

1 Who refuses to fight anybody except Macbeth himself?

2 Who becomes King of Scotland?

3 What has Lady Macbeth been seen to do on previous occasions when sleepwalking?

4 What does the doctor say of Lady Macbeth's condition?

5 Where are Young Siward's wounds, and why is this important?

6 Where exactly is Macbeth's castle (previously referred to as Inverness), and why is this significant?

7 Why, according to Macbeth, does he no longer start at the sound of cries?

8 Why is Macbeth reluctant to fight Macduff?

9 How does Birnam Wood come to Dunsinane?

10 How is Macduff able to kill Macbeth despite the prophecies?

Open quotes

Find the line – and complete the phrase or sentence.

1 'Here's the smell of the blood still...'

2 'And that which should accompany old age...'

3 'Tomorrow and tomorrow and tomorrow...'

4 'I pull in resolution...'

5 'And be those juggling fiends...'

General question on the whole play

Use the following phrase as a memory aid. List all the themes you can think of in the play that start with each letter.

MACBETH SOLD

Writing essays

- To prepare for an exam, you should read the text in full *at least* twice, preferably *three* times. You need to know it very well.

- If your text is to be studied for an 'open book' exam, make sure that you take your book with you. However, you should not rely too much on the book – you haven't got time. If you are not allowed to take the text with you, you will need to memorise brief quotations.

- You need to decide fairly swiftly about which question to answer. Choose a question which best allows you to demonstrate your understanding and personal ideas.

- Make sure you understand exactly what the question is asking you to do.

- **Plan** your answer (see page 75).

- Always have a short introduction, giving an overview of the topic. Refer to your plan as you write to ensure you keep on task. Divide your ideas into paragraphs; without them you may not get above a D grade. Try to leave time for a brief conclusion.

- Remember: **point–quotation–comment:**
  The witches talk in riddles and use oxymoron [**point**], declaring 'fair is foul and foul is fair' [**quotation**]. This shows that while their words and predictions seem to make sense, what they are actually saying depends on the interpretation of the listener [**comment**].

- The key word in writing essays in exams is **timing**. You must know how long you have for each question and stick to this.

- Leave yourself a few minutes to check through your work. It does not look impressive if you misspell the names of characters, settings or the author.

- Timing is not so crucial for coursework essays, so this is your chance to show what you can really do, without having to write under pressure.

- You can obviously go into far more detail than you are able to in an examination. You should aim for about 1000 words, but your teacher will advise you further.

- If you have a choice of title, make sure you select one that grabs your interest and gives you a lot of opportunity to develop your ideas.

- **Plan** your work (see page 75). Make sure that you often refer to the plan and the title as you write, to check that you are not drifting off course.

- Use quotations frequently but carefully and try to introduce them smoothly. It is often effective to quote just one or two words: The first mention of Macbeth is a positive one and he is hailed as 'brave', 'valiant' and a 'worthy gentleman'.

- Try to state your own opinion with phrases such as 'This suggests to me …'. You will be credited for your ideas, as long as you explain why you think them.

- Putting the play in context is very important. Include relevant background detail and explain how the cultural and historical setting affects the writer's choice of language.

- Make sure that you include a short conclusion, by summing up your key ideas.

- Don't be tempted to copy large chunks of essays available on the Internet. Your teacher will immediately notice what you have done and will not reward it.

- It is a good idea, if possible, to word process your essay. This will enable you to make changes and improvements to your final draft more easily.

Writing essays

> **"*Fair is foul and foul is fair*"** *(Act 1, Scene 1)*

This line indicates the way in which the witches speak in riddles and paradoxical statements. It can be used in an essay about the supernatural or about Macbeth (as he virtually echoes this line when he first appears on stage).

> **"*Too full o' th' milk of human kindness*"** *(Act 1, Scene 5)*

This line is important because it tells us about Macbeth's character. Although he is a great warrior, he is sensitive and caring. Use this quotation in a character essay, or even to examine the changes in Macbeth from the start to the end of the play.

> **"*False face must hide what the false heart doth know*"** *(Act 1, Scene 7)*

Lady Macbeth has warned her husband that he must pretend to be honourable and loyal when, in fact, he has murderous intentions. This line emphasises the difference between appearance and reality that runs though the play.

> **"*unsex me here*"** *(Act 1, Scene 5)*

Lady Macbeth delivers these words after receiving Macbeth's letter. This conjures an image of a character calling to the supernatural world to make her hard and ruthless. There are lots of references to male and female qualities in the play and this is a key reference. It could be used in an essay on Lady Macbeth or on the influence of the supernatural.

"Blood will have blood" *(Act 3, Scene 4)*

Macbeth cries this line after seeing Banquo's ghost in the banquet scene. It is a good example of the blood image that occurs throughout the play, but it also carries the notion of prediction. Macbeth is right – the blood he has spilled will only lead to more bloodshed.

"By the pricking of my thumbs / Something wicked this way comes" *(Act 4, Scene 1)*

This is a useful quotation to remember because it shows the way that Macbeth and the witches are inextricably linked. They sense when he is near, and he cannot resist their temptation. The fact that he is referred to as wicked is significant and could be used in a character-based essay or a thematic one based on the supernatural.

"Macbeth doth murder sleep, the innocent sleep" *(Act 2, Scene 2)*

Spoken by Macbeth after his slaughter of the king, sleep here is used as a metaphor for innocence and purity. The good at heart can find peace in sleep, but those who are evil are condemned to find no rest. This would be an excellent line to use in an essay about either Macbeth or Lady Macbeth, or on the recurring images used in the play.

"This dead butcher and his fiend-like queen" *(Act 5, Scene 9)*

This is one of the most significant lines in the play and would be essential in any essay looking at the characters and development of either Macbeth or Lady Macbeth.

Exam questions

1. *'This dead butcher and his fiend-like queen.' To what extent is this a fair comment on the characters of Macbeth and Lady Macbeth?*

2. *Justify how far we can hold Macbeth fully responsible for the evil deeds committed in the play.*

3. *Imagine you are Macbeth writing to your wife from the battlefield. Explain how the battle went, your thoughts on the traitor Cawdor and your loyal friend Banquo, and the meeting with the witches.*

4. *How wicked is Lady Macbeth?*

5. *Explore the significance of the role played by the supernatural in* Macbeth.

6. Macbeth *is a play about murder and killing. What kinds of death are featured in the play and how does Shakespeare portray their differences, dramatically?*

7. *In Act 1, Scene 1, the Captain gives news of the victory against the Norwegians to King Duncan. Write his official report of the battle. Remember to include details about the enemy attack, the treacherous behaviour of the Thane of Cawdor, as well as of Macbeth's bravery and the eventual victory.*

8. *You are Macbeth. Write a diary entry, detailing your thoughts after meeting the weird sisters and then being awarded the title 'Thane of Cawdor'.*

9. *Explore the importance of sleep and sleep imagery in the play.*

10. *Who is responsible for the eventual downfall of Macbeth?*

11. *How does Shakespeare use soliloquy to reveal character? Choose two examples from the play and explain how they develop character.*

12. *Discuss the relationship between Macbeth and his wife. How does this relationship change during the course of the play, and why do you think this is?*

13 Explore the theme of nature in the play.

14 How well does the opening scene prepare the audience for the themes and imagery contained within the rest of the play?

15 Shakespeare uses many contrasting ideas in Macbeth. How is the notion of contrast used to develop character, themes and motifs in the play?

16 Discuss the changes in Lady Macbeth's character and explore why she continues to fascinate audiences today.

17 Explore the role of the various women in Macbeth.

18 Act 3, Scene 4 – the banquet scene which features Banquo's ghost – is dramatically rich. As a director, what decisions would you make about the staging of this scene and what advice would you give to the actors?

19 Discuss how the theme of appearance versus reality is explored in Macbeth.

20 The story of Macbeth is a typical tragedy – a great man is brought down by a fatal flaw. How far do you agree with this view of the play?

21 Consider the ways in which the recurring imagery within Macbeth adds to the power of the play.

Spidergrams for questions 5, 6 and 10 are shown on pages 75–77.

It is very important to be organised in your approach. Time spent in planning your response will be reflected in the grade you receive.

- The first thing to do is to read the question very carefully to make sure you fully understand it, and then highlight key words.

- You will need to make some notes on the topic to help you. This can be done in various ways: a list; subheadings; a spider diagram; or a mind map.

- The advantage of using a spidergram is that it lets you expand your ideas in a clearly linked, visual way. Put the essay title in the centre of the page. From this a number of key ideas will come out in the form of branches.

- By focusing on each key idea in turn, you will be able to branch out further, as your brain makes connections between the ideas.

- Since a spidergram is a way of charting your knowledge, it is also an excellent revision aid. You could work through a number of essay titles in this way.

- Some people prefer to make a spidergram even more visual, by colour coding ideas and even adding pictures or symbols.

- In the planning stage of an essay, it is a good idea to jot down some useful quotations. These need not be lengthy and can be added to your spidergram.

- Each branch of a spidergram might form a separate paragraph in your essay. You can number the branches, so that you are clear about the order of your points. Deal with the main points first.

Some pupils say that they do not like planning and that they never do so, but the majority of candidates do significantly better when they plan their answers.

Spidergram essay plans

Who is responsible for the eventual downfall of Macbeth?

Lady Macbeth
- character
  - determined
  - ruthless
  - persuasive
    - attacks his manliness
    - calls him a coward
    - 'was the hope drunk?'
- role of wife
  - supportive
  - desire to be Queen?

witches
- 'a drum, a drum, Macbeth doth come'
- play with the lives of men
- meddle with fate and destiny
  - audience expectations
- Act 4 contribution to downfall
- dramatic effect
  - spells
  - appearance

Macbeth's character
- start of play
  - ambitious
  - brutal warrior
  - hero
- after Duncan's death
  - 'bloody tyrant'
  - becomes independent
    - 'be innocent of the knowledge'
  - prepared to murder anyone in his way
    - guards
    - Lady Macduff
    - Banquo

Duncan's murder
- no going back
  - 'We are yet but young in deed'
- destroyed the natural order
  - 'if chance will have me king, chance will crown me'
- seed sown by witches, executed by Macbeth

75

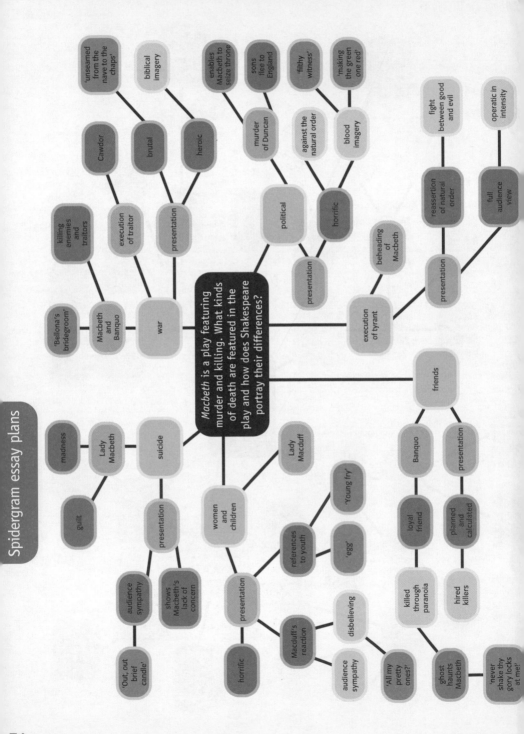

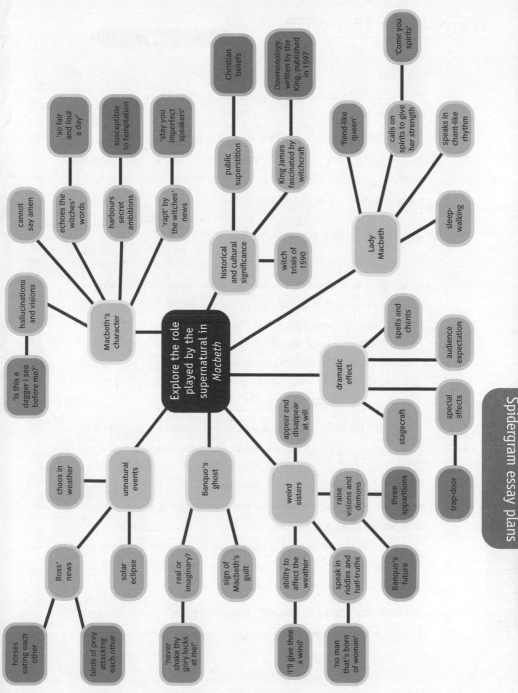

Explore the role played by the supernatural in *Macbeth*

Macbeth's character
- cannot say amen
- echoes the witches' words
- hallucinations and visions
  - 'Is this a dagger I see before me?'
- harbours secret ambitions
- 'rapt' by the witches' news
- 'so fair and foul a day'
- susceptible to temptation
- 'stay you imperfect speakers'

historical and cultural significance
- public superstition
  - Christian beliefs
  - *Daemonology*, written by the King, published in 1597
- King James fascinated by witchcraft
- witch trials of 1590

Lady Macbeth
- 'fiend-like queen'
- calls on spirits to give her strength
  - 'Come you spirits'
- speaks in chant-like rhythm
- sleep-walking

dramatic effect
- spells and chants
- audience expectation
- special effects
  - trap-door
- stagecraft

weird sisters
- appear and disappear at will
- raise visions and demons
  - three apparitions
- ability to affect the weather
  - 'I'll give thee a wind'
- speak in riddles and half-truths
  - 'no man that's born of woman'
- Banquo's future

unnatural events
- chaos in weather
- Ross' news
  - horses eating each other
  - birds of prey attacking each other
- solar eclipse

Banquo's ghost
- real or imaginary?
  - 'never shake thy gory locks at me!'
- sign of Macbeth's guilt

Spidergram essay plans

77

Sample response

How does Lady Macbeth convince Macbeth to kill the king in Act 1, Scene 7?

This scene comes after Macbeth has seen the witches and been told that he will become king. He wrote a letter to his wife and explained what happened, and they decided that he needed to kill the king. Lady Macbeth knows that her husband is probably too nice to go through with the murder so she tries to persuade him that he needs to be strong and manly. ✔

She starts by asking him 'was the hope drunk wherein you dressed yourself?' This means that she thinks he was drunk and not being clear-headed when he earlier suggested that he kill his king. She asks him if it is 'green and pale', which makes me think she is accusing him of being feeble and scared. If you are nervous and frightened you would probably be shaking and white. ✔ Lady Macbeth accuses him of being too timid to go for what he wants and asks him if he is 'afeard' to do something to make his dreams come true.

Lady Macbeth uses very brutal imagery to compare herself to her husband and explains that she would never say she would do something and then not go through with it. ✔ She talks about killing a baby and says, 'I know how tender 'tis to love the babe that milks me'. This means that even though she is a woman, she would still rather kill her own baby than go back on her word. ✔ The fact that she uses this horrible image shows that she is stronger than Macbeth. This would probably make him ashamed. ✔ This would also be shocking to the audience.

Macbeth looks to Lady Macbeth to make him feel better and to tell him what would happen if things go wrong. This shows that she can calm him down by giving him reassurance. She gives him a long list of practical things that she will take care of, like waiting until Duncan is asleep and giving his grooms lots of alcohol to drink so they will fall unconscious. ✔

By the end of the scene Macbeth is obviously feeling better and more determined because he says that Lady Macbeth should only have 'men-children' because they are stronger. In his final couplet ✔ he says that 'false face must hide what the false heart doth know'. This shows that he has been convinced because he is using a similar image to the one Lady Macbeth used in the previous scene when she tells him that he must look like a 'flower' but be the 'serpent' underneath it. ✔✔

In this scene Lady Macbeth manages to convince her husband because she firstly accuses him of being a coward, then she explains how she could do it, to make him feel ashamed. She also stops him worrying about the practical details of the murder, so by the end he is ready to go through with the deed. ✔

Examiner's comments

This is a balanced response which is closely focused on the title. Quotations are used appropriately, illustrating that this candidate understands the author's craft. There is a little straying into telling the story in the introduction and the points, although accurate, are not developed enough. This candidate shows a personal engagement with the text and understands authorial intent. There is language focus but there needs to be more reference to the drama within the scene and to the dramatisation of the characters. The response is clearly structured with an introduction and a conclusion.

Sample response

How does Lady Macbeth convince Macbeth to kill the king in Act 1, Scene 7?

In this scene Lady Macbeth uses different powers of persuasion to encourage her husband to kill King Duncan. She knows he is aware that murder is the only way to make the witches' predictions come true, but she also believes that Macbeth might be 'too full o' th' milk of human kindness'. Here, she uses several techniques to stiffen his resolve.

She begins by asking him, 'was the hope drunk wherein you dressed yourself?' She uses the metaphor of alcohol to imply that his courage and bravado was the result of intoxication and not genuine determination. ✔ Macbeth is a great warrior, and the audience has already heard of his brutal fighting skills, so by accusing him of being a drunken show-off, she will be offending his manliness. ✔ She takes this image further by accusing him of being feeble and scared: 'green and pale'. She also accuses him of being too timid and 'afeard' to do something to make his dreams come true. Macbeth has probably never been accused of being a coward, so this would be a very effective technique. ✔✔

Lady Macbeth then uses very brutal imagery, juxtaposing herself with her husband. ✔ She declares that she would never say she would do something and then not go through with it. ✔ She talks about killing her own baby and says, 'I know how tender 'tis to love the babe that milks me'. This means that even though she is a woman, she would still rather kill her own baby than go back on her word. By using an image suffused with tenderness and sensitivity, with words such as 'milk', 'suck', 'smiling' and then brutally contrasting this with verbs such as 'plucked' and 'dashed' she creates a horribly violent image, which shows that she is stronger than Macbeth. ✔✔ This would make him ashamed and would also be shocking to the audience.

Lady Macbeth also focuses on his manliness and strikes at his male pride saying, 'then you were a man'. She knows that her husband would be moved by this accusation and would want to prove to her that he is still a strong warrior and husband. He would not want to let her down. ✔

Macbeth looks to his wife to make him feel better and to tell him what would happen if things went wrong. When he talks about failing, she says, 'we fail?' The actress playing this part would probably say this as if she is full of disbelief and would not even begin to consider their plan going wrong. This would show Macbeth that he needs to think positively and not dwell on the negative. ✔✔

Lady Macbeth calms her husband down by giving him reassurance and explaining all the practical considerations that she has already taken care of, such as drugging the grooms and ensuring they are free to do the deed. I notice that she is also careful not to mention the actual word murder anywhere in this scene. She calls it 'great quell', which is an example of euphemism. ✔ By not calling it what it is, it does not seem so bad, and the word 'great' even suggests that what they are doing is a brave and honourable thing. ✔✔

By the end of the scene, Macbeth is obviously feeling stronger and in his final couplet he says that 'false face must hide what the false heart doth know'. This shows that he has been convinced because

Sample responses

he is using a similar image to the one Lady Macbeth used in the previous scene when she tells him that he must look like a 'flower' but be the 'serpent' underneath it. ✓

In this scene Lady Macbeth manages to convince her husband by accusing him of being a coward, asking lots of rhetorical questions to make him think of the consequences, using herself as a comparison to question his gender, and explaining how she could do it to make him feel ashamed. She also stops him worrying about the practical details of the murder, so by the end he has no reason not to go through with their plans. ✓

Examiner's comments

This is a very strong answer which is well structured and closely focused on the title. Quotations are used in interesting ways to support the candidate's ideas and there is a confidence in interpretation. Linguistically, this candidate understands authorial intention as well as dramatisation of the characters. There is clear appreciation of this scene as a piece of drama, and consideration is given to audience and purpose. Good contextual understanding is shown and original and interesting links are made.

Quick quiz answers

Quick quiz 1
Who? What? Where? When? Why? How?

1   Malcolm, Prince of Cumberland
2   the witches
3   He is Thane of Glamis and Thane of Cawdor. He is promised the title King of Scotland.
4   withered, wild clothes, women but bearded
5   on a blasted heath
6   As Macbeth is 'full of the milk of human kindness', she is afraid this may prevent him from seizing the crown.
7   Duncan is Macbeth's kinsman, his king, his guest and a virtuous man. Macbeth has been newly honoured by him and does not want to lose his political favour yet.
8   drug them; blame them by using their daggers and splashing them with blood

Open quotes

1   'Stars, hide your fires; / Let not light see my black and deep desires.'
2   'Thou wouldst be great, / Art not without ambition, but without / The illness should attend it.'
3   'That but this blow / Might be the be-all and the end-all here / But here upon this bank and shoal of time.'
4   'I have no spur / To prick the sides of my intent, but only / Vaulting ambition.'
5   'We fail! / But screw your courage to the sticking-place / And we'll not fail.'

Imperfect speakers?

1   He will be lesser and greater than Macbeth, not so happy and yet happier, and the father of kings, though no king himself.
2   The audience knows that part of the prediction has already come true, and that the witches have been waiting for Macbeth. Banquo says that their predictions 'sound so fair', but how trustworthy are they?
3   Banquo suspects that this may be an 'honest trifle' – a small piece of truth – to lead them on to betrayal.
4   It cannot be ill because there is some truth in it already. It cannot be good because he is already horrified at how his mind is working.

Quick quiz 2
Who? What? Where? When? Why? How?

1   Banquo and Fleance, joined by Macbeth
2   Banquo, because in repose he starts thinking about the witches' words
3   Lennox tells of storms: chimneys blown down, the air filled with screams and voices, owls screeching, the earth shaking. Ross and the Old Man speak of unnatural dark, an owl killing a

falcon and Duncan's horses eating one another.

4 Macbeth sees a dagger, its handle towards his hand. Either it is leading him to kill Duncan, or his thoughts of killing Duncan have produced it.

5 England and Ireland respectively

6 Scone; Macduff (who is the local Thane)

7 to prevent their denials; in a rage that they have killed Duncan; Lady Macbeth faints

8 because he resembles her father in sleep

9 the bell is the summons to heaven or hell; the knocking cannot wake Duncan

10 they are about stealing, equivocating and self-destructive ambition/ expectations

Open quotes

1 'Or art thou but a dagger of the mind, a false creation / Proceeding from the heat-oppressed brain?'

2 'But wherefore could not I pronounce 'Amen'? / I had most need of blessing and 'Amen' / Stuck in my throat.'

3 'Will all great Neptune's ocean wash this blood / Clean from my hand?'

4 'There's nothing serious in mortality – / All is but toys; renown and grace is dead.'

5 ''Tis unnatural, / Even like the deed that's done.'

Night moves

There are lots of examples. Here are just a few suggestions.

1 'The sleeping and the dead / Are but as pictures'; 'Sleep…The death of each day's life'; 'Shake off this downy sleep, death's counterfeit, / And look on death itself!'

2 'Methought I heard a voice cry: "Sleep no more; Macbeth does murder sleep"; 'A heavy summons lies like lead upon me / And yet I would not sleep.'; 'Macbeth shall sleep no more'.

3 'The bell invites me…it is a knell / That summons thee to heaven or to hell.'; 'Here's a knocking indeed!'; 'Wake Duncan with thy knocking! I would thou couldst!'

4 'I dreamt last night of the three Weird Sisters.'; 'Wicked dreams abuse / The curtained sleep'; 'There's one did laugh in's sleep, and one cried 'Murder!' / That they did wake each other.'

Quick quiz 3

Who? What? Where? When? Why? How?

1 Banquo; he does indeed turn up, but as a ghost

2 'a fruitless crown' and 'a barren sceptre'

3 scarce food, no sleep, violence, cut-throat politics and dishonesty

4 in England; asking Edward for help to overthrow Macbeth; the banquet

5 already at court for the banquet
6 because he thinks all the places are full – his chair is occupied by the ghost
7 because he is at rest, safe in his grave
8 Banquo's honesty, courage and wisdom are dangerous; Banquo's children will rob him of the throne; Banquo is blamed for the murderers' poverty.
9 He tries to ignore it, in case his hopes are raised, which he recognises as temptation.

Open quotes
1 'Thou hast it now: King, Cawdor, Glamis / All as the weird women promised; and I fear / Thou play'dst most foully for't.'
2 'To be thus is nothing / But to be safely thus. Our fears in Banquo / Stick deep'
3 'Naught's had, all's spent / Where our desire is got without content.'
4 'I am in blood / Stepped in so far that, should I wade no more / Returning were as tedious as go o-er.'
5 'Better be with the dead / Whom we, to gain our peace, have sent to peace, / Than on the torture of the mind to lie.'

Creature features?
1 snake, scorpion, bat, beetle, crow
2 Fleance (son of 'the grown serpent' Banquo)
3 Russian bear, arm'd rhinoceros, Hyrcanian tiger

Quick quiz 4
Who? What? Where? When? Why? How?
1 Macbeth
2 Ross (who later has to bring the news to Macduff)
3 'Justice, verity, temperence, stableness, / Bounty, perseverence, courage, fortitude.'
4 to march on Scotland with 10,000 men under Old Siward
5 in a dark cave
6 Macbeth was once honest; Macduff loved Macbeth well; Macduff has not yet been harmed by Macbeth
7 because 'The night is long that never finds the day'
8 by killing off Macduff's family – this doesn't make him safer from Macduff, whom it spurs to revenge

Open quotes
1 'Be bloody, bold and resolute: laugh to scorn / The pow'r of man, for none of woman born / Shall harm Macbeth.'
2 'No boasting like a fool. / This deed I'll do before this purpose cool.'
3 'Angels are bright still, though the brightest fell.'
4 'Each new morn / New widows howl, new orphans cry.'
5 'Macbeth is ripe for shaking and the pow'rs above / Put on their instruments.'

A matter of trust

1   (a) the armed head – could be
    neutral, or Macduff, or Macbeth's
    own end
    (b) the bloody child – encourages
    false security (Macduff is not, in
    fact of woman born); Macbeth
    takes it as a reminder to kill
    more children!
    (c) the child crowned, with tree –
    its message about Birnam wood
    sounds impossible but does in
    fact come true; it may represent
    Malcolm or Banquo's heirs
2   Macbeth; because he has
    trusted them and is damned.
3   Ross and Lady Macduff
    (because he has left country
    and family); the murderers
    (instructed by Macbeth);
    Malcolm (to test his loyalty)
4   Macduff
5   because 'Such welcome and
    unwelcome things at once /
    Tis hard to reconcile.' Macbeth
    knows this feeling: he will be
    king but his heirs will not.

Quick quiz 5

Who? What? Where? When? Why?
How?
1   Macduff
2   Malcolm
3   She walks with a candle, eyes
    open, writes on a paper, seals it
    and returns to bed.
4   She needs a priest (divine), not
    a doctor. She needs to cleanse
    her conscience – this is not a
    physical illness.

5   in the front; because this shows
    he has been fighting, not fleeing
6   Dunsinane; this is in the
    prophecy of his defeat
7   because he has 'supped full
    of horrors', 'direness' is familiar
    to him
8   because he has shed too much
    of his family's blood already
9   Branches from the wood are
    used as camouflage for the
    soldiers' approach to the castle.
10 He was not born of woman, but
    was taken early from his
    mother's womb.

Open quotes

1   'Here's the smell of the blood
    still...All the perfumes of
    Arabia will not sweeten this
    little hand.'
2   'And that which should
    accompany old age, / As honour,
    love, obedience, troops of
    friends / I must not look to have.'
3   'Tomorrow and tomorrow
    and tomorrow, / Creeps in
    this petty pace from day to
    day / To the last syllable of
    recorded time.'
4   'I pull in resolution and begin /
    To doubt th'equivocation of the
    fiend / That lies like truth.'
5   'And be those juggling fiends no
    more believ'd / That palter with
    us in a double sense.'

General question on the whole play
Here are some suggestions:

M murder, morality, madness, medicine

A ambition, ambiguity, animals

C clothing, chaos, children, conscience, crown, cowardice, curse, courage

B blood, bravery, bathing

E equivocation, evil

T time, trust, tiredness, tyranny

H hospitality, hesitation, holiness, horror, health, honesty, honour, hope

S sleep, sickness, storms, state, savagery, sleeplessness, safety, supernatural, seeds

O order

L light, loyalty

D deception, determination, dreams, damnation, doom, disorder, darkness, death, doubt, divine right of kings

Page 18, Shakespeare, © Robert Harding World Imagery/
Robert Harding Picture Library/Alamy.Com
Page 21, Scene, © Robbie Jack/Corbis

Every effort has been made to trace copyright holders and to obtain their
permission for the use of copyright material. The author and the publisher
will gladly receive information enabling them to rectify any reference or
credit in subsequent editions.

Published by Letts Educational
An imprint of HarperCollins*Publishers*
77–85 Fulham Palace Road
London W6 8JB

Phone orders: 0844 576 8126
Fax orders: 0844 576 8131
Email: education@harpercollins.co.uk
Website: www.lettsrevision.com

ISBN 978 1 84315 311 5

First published 1994
Revised edition 2004

01/140611
10 9 8 7 6

Text © John Mahoney and Stewart Martin 1994
2004 edition revised by Clare Crane

Design and illustration © Letts Educational

British Library Cataloguing in Publication Data. A CIP record of this book is
available from the British Library.

Cover and text design by Hardlines Ltd, Charlbury, Oxfordshire.

Typeset by Letterpart Ltd, Reigate, Surrey.

Graphic illustration by Beehive Illustration, Cirencester, Gloucestershire.

Commissioned by Cassandra Birmingham

Editorial project management by Vicky Butt

Printed in China

MIX
Paper from
responsible sources

FSC
www.fsc.org
FSC™ C007454

FSC™ is a non-profit international organisation established to promote the
responsible management of the world's forests. Products carrying the FSC
label are independently certified to assure consumers that they come from
forests that are managed to meet the social, economic and ecological needs
of present and future generations, and other controlled sources.

Find out more about HarperCollins and the environment at
www.harpercollins.co.uk/green